How to Raise Inclusive Children

Copyright

While every precaution has been taken in the preparation of this book, the publisher assumes no responsibility for errors or omissions, or for damages resulting from the use of the information contained herein.

How to Raise Inclusive Children

Copyright © 2025 Trish Allison

All rights reserved. No part of this book may be used or reproduced in any manner whatsoever without written permission from the author.

ISBN: 978-0-9998486-8-5

First edition. June 2025

NO AI TRAINING: Without in any way limiting the author's (and publisher's) exclusive rights under copyright, any use of this publication to "train" generative artificial intelligence (AI) technologies to generate text is expressly prohibited. The author reserves all rights to license uses of this work for generative AI training and development of machine learning language models.

Table of Contents

How to Raise Inclusive Children (DEI Parent Guidebooks, #13) 1

Introduction 5

Section I. DEI Communication with Kids 9

Chapter 1. | Answering Kids' Questions 11

Chapter 2. | Stereotypes 15

Chapter 3. | Allies 21

Chapter 4. | Household Adjustments 27

Chapter 5. | Find Out What Your Child Already Knows 33

Section II. | Individual DEI Subjects 41

Chapter 6. | Immigration 43

Chapter 7. | Transgender 53

Chapter 8. | Poverty 63

Chapter 9. | LGBTQ+ 75

Chapter 10. | Girls 85

Chapter 11. | Boys 147

Chapter 12. | Religion 181

Chapter 13. | Older People 193

Chapter 14. | Indigenous Americans 211

Chapter 15. | Disability 223

Chapter 16. | ASD Siblings 239

Chapter 17. | Cultural Diversity 249

Reference Notes 267

"Children are the architects of tomorrow's world."

TRISH ALLISON

How to Use This Guidebook

We divided this book into 2 sections. Section 1 offers general communication tips for discussing sensitive topics with kids. Section 2 provides separate chapters for individual DEI subjects. Our suggestion is to read all of Section 1, and then cherry pick individual Section 2 chapters that apply specifically to your family.

Instead of sit-down lectures about what your child should believe, our approach is to help you plant seeds of information. Kids learn best when they can apply given information to events in their own world, decide if it makes sense or not, and ultimately feel like they formulated an opinion on their own.

We tailored each suggestion for parents/caregivers of elementary-school-age kids. That said, we're fully aware there are vastly different maturity levels at every age, and parents know best what is and isn't appropriate for their own child.

None of the steps in this guidebook are intended to be completed on a single, dictatorial occasion. Instead, the goal is to sporadically communicate the values described here on a casual basis, over a period of time.

As you're reading, keep in mind that our step-by-step guidance is a starting point ONLY. Please customize our suggestions to align with your personal family values.

With busy parents in mind, this guidebook provides the most amount of information using the least amount of words possible. Each chapter uses a step-by-step approach with succinct instructions you can use immediately.

HOW TO RAISE INCLUSIVE CHILDREN

Introduction

Our world is growing increasingly troubled, with a moneyed few in power and entire populations wrongly shunned and plagued by poverty.

That means it's more important than ever for parents to proactively raise a generation of equality-minded humans who can thrive in a fairer future.

The best way to do that is to guide kids toward compassion and respect for *all* different types of people by giving them accurate information.

For example, they need to know that transgender people are just as worthy of respect as cisgender white males. Gay men and lesbians are just as valid and honorable as heterosexuals.

Women are not inferior. Homeless people didn't do anything wrong.

ALL humans are equal. Period.

Kids need to know this.

We decided to focus on elementary-school-age kids because their cognitive abilities have progressed enough to understand concepts like groups and fairness.

This is a crucial age group for introducing fundamental words and actions that support diversity, equity, and inclusion. That said, there are different maturity levels at every age. We get that.

TRISH ALLISON

Parents know best what is and isn't appropriate for their own child. Please adjust the ideas in this book to fit your child's personal level of development.

The ultimate goal here is to help you raise compassionate, unbiased, successful humans who embrace the significance of "justice for all."

So, to the parents worried their kids could grow up without a solid understanding of DEI principles, this book is for you.

HOW TO RAISE INCLUSIVE CHILDREN

Section I. DEI Communication with Kids

In Chapters 1-5, we discuss the fundamentals of DEI communication with kids.

We'll go over how to answer kids' questions, clarify stereotypes, discuss how and when to be an ally, make household adjustments, and how to find out what your child already knows.

TRISH ALLISON

Chapter 1.
Answering Kids' Questions

The more accepting our society (eventually!) becomes toward all types of people, the more questions kids will ask. It's actually a good thing.

The trick is answering their questions with small, accurate nuggets of information that steer them toward formulating their own conclusions—critical thinking in action!

Why do kids ask so many questions?

It's inevitable that your child will ask lots of questions. It's how they learn about the world around them.

Be prepared to field questions at potentially embarrassing moments.

As we all know, kids are unpredictable and often ask embarrassing questions in public.

According to the article, "**Answering Your Child's Toughest Questions,**" *"If your child asks you an embarrassing question when you're out in public, answer as honestly as you can, sticking to facts and avoiding imposing your judgments. Again, you will want to speak softly, suggesting that it's best to ask questions that might make someone uncomfortable when that person isn't nearby."* [1]

The good news is that by learning how to answer your child compassionately and accurately, you'll be contributing to the (eventual) progress of becoming a truly inclusive society.

Give direct and simple answers

Evading questions about controversial subjects gives your child the impression that there's something inherently evil about the subject and it shouldn't be discussed.

The major risk here is that your child will create their own answer with potentially erroneous information.

> Instead, offer a simple, straightforward answer.
>
> This will send a crucial message to your child that diversity and inclusion topics are not shameful. Try to look as comfortable as possible during these exchanges—as if you're discussing the grocery list.
>
> Even if you're not comfortable, fake it. If you're anxious, your child will read into it and assume there's something wrong with talking about it.
>
> Aim for an open, educational tone. Your attitude shapes theirs. If you don't know the answer to the question, be honest and admit that you don't know. Look it up online together.
>
> Just as important as "not dodging questions" is providing answers that are simple. Kids learn best by processing the information we give them and then applying it to their own world. This is especially true for nuanced concepts like fairness.
>
> Children who feel like they learned a concept with their *own* reasoning skills are much more apt to translate that concept into a long-term personal value.

The simpler the answer to their question, the easier it is for them to process the information. They don't need any information beyond what they're specifically asking.

So, when/if your child asks, *"Why is that man wearing a dress?"* You don't need to offer any explanation beyond, *"He probably likes it."*

Or if your child asks, *"Can people in wheelchairs drive cars?"* The only response you need to provide is *"Yes, cars can be modified to allow people who can't use their legs to use hand controls instead."* Period.

The big-picture goal is to provide simple responses that answer the question directly and subtly guide them toward formulating their own opinion.

Embrace teachable moments

Teachable moments are perfect for offering simple, direct answers. From song lyrics to TV to meeting people in the community, there are lots of chances to start a conversation about justice for marginalized people.

Also, teachable moments can take the pressure off of both you and your child because part of the focus is on the event itself, and not fully on the conversation.

TRISH ALLISON

In "Teachable Moments in Your Everyday Life," we learn, "These moments are hiding everywhere during everyday life ... from your daily car ride and a stop at the store, to meal prep and household chores. The key is in slowing down and being aware of the opportunities as they arise!" [2]

By seizing these unplanned instances, you can connect abstract principles to concrete situations, making lessons about empathy and fairness far more impactful and memorable than formal lectures.

Chapter 2.
Stereotypes

Stereotypes are a huge roadblock to respecting marginalized people. It's crucial to help your child grasp how stereotypes work.

The first goal of this chapter is to help your child understand what stereotypes are, how they're used in everyday life, and how damaging they can be.

Next, you'll find stereotype examples to help you get your message across effectively. We also intentionally provided examples that *defy* common stereotypes to end your child's understanding of stereotypes on a positive note.

Define stereotypes

Start your discussion by first making sure your child knows what stereotypes are. Instead of putting them on the spot and quizzing them about the definition of a stereotype, offer your own definition:

"Stereotyping is assuming that everyone is alike. It's looking at a whole group of people and assuming that they all share the same qualities."

Try to limit your conversation to a definition of "stereotypes." At this point, talking about "big picture" issues like misplaced anger and hate crimes could be distracting and counterproductive.

Instead, first make sure your child fully understands what stereotypes are before moving on to more complicated concepts.

Explain why stereotypes are harmful

Once you feel like your child understands what stereotypes are, explain why they're so harmful.

A simple way to communicate this is to say that stereotypes can hurt people's feelings and create feelings of worthlessness.

The harmful effects of stereotyping can be an abstract concept for children to absorb. But it's an important one to teach because it can be so pervasive and damaging.

The National Institute of Health explains "Stereotype threat appears to impair performance by inducing physiological stress and by prompting attempts at both behavioral and emotional regulation—all of which, independently or in concert, have the effect of consuming cognitive resources needed for intellectual functioning."[3]

Remember that this isn't necessarily about specific stereotypes. You're just trying to explain the harmful effects of stereotypes *in general*.

If possible, offer a scenario that pertains to you.

For example, suppose you were passed by for a promotion at your job even though you were clearly the most qualified. Explain that the hiring manager just assumed you weren't qualified because of your race or gender.

Talk about how it made you feel (temporarily!) like there was no point in trying.

If you have a similar story you can share, this is a really good way to help your child understand how damaging stereotypes can be. Kids love to hear personal stories about their parents.

Or maybe you *witnessed* the effects of someone else being stereotyped. Whether you saw it, heard it, experienced it, dreamed it, whatever—it won't matter to your child. It's just the concept of stereotype damage that you're trying to convey.

Hopefully, they'll chime in here and offer their own example of a stereotype that's hurtful. If/when they do, be sure to listen attentively and praise them for understanding such a complicated concept so well.

Before moving on to the next section, make sure your child has a solid understanding of how damaging stereotypes can be.

Stereotype Examples

Now that you've discussed stereotypes in general and how damaging they can be, pivot the conversation to stereotype *examples*.

Transgender people, immigrants, and poor people are, unfortunately, blatantly stereotyped populations that might be effective for getting your point across.

Transgender stereotype examples. Talking about transgender stereotypes is a good way to get your child engaged in the discussion about stereotypes if they aren't already.

Start the process by Googling phrases like "common transgender stereotypes."

Click on the search result that you think will both engage your child and also fall within their current stage of development. Talk about what you find with your child.

Keep the conversation going. Look up another transgender stereotype and talk about it. Do you know anyone personally who has been persecuted because of their gender identity?

Without providing gory details, mention that for centuries, transgender people have been stereotyped as freaks and treated with emotional and social isolation and even violence.

Immigrant stereotype examples. One of the common misconceptions about immigrants is that they refuse to learn the language of their new country.

Not true.

The article "Ten Myths About Immigration" clarifies this erroneous idea, "Immigrants must speak, read, write, and understand the English language, not only for the naturalization application process, but also so they can pass a 100-question civics test that has both oral and written components." [4]

While many immigrants do speak their native language when they're in their own home, most make a concerted effort to speak the language of their new country when they're out in public.

Another common inaccurate stereotype about immigrants is that they take good jobs from existing citizens.

Again, not true.

Research shows that immigrants rarely take native workers' jobs.

Like all stereotypes, a few bad apples spoil the reputation of the whole bunch. Yes, there are some immigrants who take advantage of their new country, but the majority of them are honest, hardworking, decent people.

Poverty stereotype examples. One of the more common stereotypes about poverty is that poor people are lazy and just need to go out and get a job.

It's sad to think that so many people assume the plight of the poor can be boiled down to a single (inaccurate) reason.

But it's a recurring theme, and it's one of the stereotypes about poverty that you should discuss with your child.

Try to dig into the *why* of this false stereotype.

Is it because people feel if they apply a single answer to the problem, they won't have to consider the myriads of reasons some people fall through the cracks of society?

Talk about it together to come up with your own reasons poor people are judged so quickly, harshly, and incorrectly.

Make sure your conversation is age appropriate.

Provide examples that DEFY stereotypes

It's time to inject some hope into this subject. The possibility of developing ongoing understanding and respect for stereotyped people should be a *hopeful* subject, not dreary.

At this point, your child should have a solid understanding of stereotypes and why they're so harmful.

It's time to expose them to as many examples as possible that *defy* stereotypes. The goal here is to help your child understand that marginalized people are just humans like all of us, and that we all have something that's different about us.

You could bring up people you think your child would recognize who grew up in poverty and went on to lead successful lives. Selena Gomez? Kelly Clarkson?

Anyone you think your child would know.

Or, depending on their age, you could talk about Disney's Moana as an example of someone who defied the stereotype that girls are weak and fearful.

Or Steven Hawking as an example of someone who defied the stereotype of disabled people as unproductive.

The idea is to give your child a *visual* of someone they recognize who defies a stereotype. You could also do an online search of "examples of people who defy stereotypes" if you need more examples.

Chapter 3.
Allies

This chapter's goal is to help you communicate the importance of being an ally and standing up for what's right.

The first thing to get across is allyship in general. Then you can help your child understand how and when it's appropriate to be an ally, including specific words and actions they can use.

Explain what it means to be an ally

First define *ally* in simple terms. To be an ally just means you're willing to stand up for someone else.

Consider offering an example of an ally here. Your child might still be processing what an ally means and needs more time to think.

You could say something like:

"I heard a story about a girl named Claire. Her friend Sophia was the child of immigrant parents from South America. They played together every day, and Claire's other friends constantly made fun of her. They tried to convince her repeatedly to play with them instead of Sophia.

Even though Claire's friends made fun of her for playing with Sophia, Claire ignored them and continued playing with her friend Sophia. That's an ally."

Note: You can substitute Claire and Sophia's names for male names if needed. Or you can make any other scenario adjustments to better fit your child's maturity level.

Gauge your child's reaction here. Is this the first time your child is grasping the concept of being an ally? Do they have a question about the scenario? If so, this is a perfect time to make sure they understand.

Discuss why and how Claire was an ally to Sophia. Even though Claire's friends made fun of her for playing with Sophia, she continued to play with her. She didn't want Sophia to be alone, plus she really liked spending time with her.

Reiterate what it means to be an ally: making it clear that you care about other people and you're willing to stand by their side. Practice at home.

Explain how and when to be an ally

As with most of the concepts discussed in this book, the best way to teach your child how and when to be an ally is by modeling the behavior yourself.

For example, if your child is out with you doing errands and you both witness an immigrant being targeted unfairly, stop what you're doing.

You don't necessarily have to be the type of ally who makes a big ugly scene and shouts obscenities, but you *do* have to stand up for what's right if your child is with you. Sometimes that involves an uncomfortable situation.

Ask questions before you step in. The situation might not be what it looks like. Or maybe it *is* what it looks like and it's appropriate for you to say something or do something.

Talk about when to step in with your child. Talk about what you did and how you knew it was the right thing to do at the time. It's an important, and sometimes abstract, distinction for children to grasp.

Not every situation warrants someone to step in. Sometimes it's better to get help from a responsible adult. Kids need to know this.

You know best how to approach the subject with your child. If needed, talk through some potential scenarios that illustrate what to do, and not do, in various situations.

Here are a few things you might talk about when discussing timing:

- If you're in a situation that you're not sure what to do in, ask yourself "Is this fair?" and "Should I offer to help or go tell someone?"

- Never put yourself in harm's way. If a situation is unsafe or if you find yourself in a situation where you need trustworthy adult supervision or help, go get it.

- Know when you're not needed to speak or stand up for someone else and step back. This could be a time when someone or a group is capable of making their own change, and they don't need external input.

The ultimate goal is to raise a child who knows when to be gutsy and can say, "Nope, that's not okay," when they spot an injustice. Or friendly enough to say, "Hi, new kid, you can sit here." Or brave enough to say, "Stop picking on her!"

Offer specific words and actions

Once you feel your child understands what it means to be an ally and importantly—when it is and isn't appropriate—it's time to offer options for specific words and actions to use.

For example, suppose your child tells you there's a kid named Lucas in the neighborhood who always gets picked last for neighborhood teams even though he's really good at sports (or whatever your child tells you).

Talk about it. Ask open-ended questions. Ask how Lucas reacts to being shunned. Ask why or why not your child thinks it's fair to him.

If someone is already doing something about it by defending Lucas, that's great. Praise that person for standing up for what they believe. Make a big deal about it.

Ask about the specific words and actions the ally used to stand up for Lucas. Ask if/how it improved the situation.

Say something about how it made you feel to hear that someone stood up for what's right. Then ask how it made your child feel.

Try to keep the conversation going here. This is a great opportunity to provide potential options for your child to respond similarly when faced with a comparable situation.

Without putting them on the spot, ask what words and/or actions they would use to come to Lucas's defense. If they need help getting started, you could say something like:

"If it were me and I saw someone being treated unfairly because of their heritage or anything else, I would say something. But only if it felt safe. I'd probably go and stand next to Lucas and say something like 'Why don't you pick Lucas for your team? He's really good at sports.'"

(Or whatever language is appropriate for your child's age.)

Giving your child a specific plan (standing next to Lucas, then using words to defend him) will hopefully give them a mental image of what it means to be an ally.

HOW TO RAISE INCLUSIVE CHILDREN

Also, your child should know that just pointing out the behavior without being accusative can sometimes be more effective than shaming the bully.

Tell your child they could say something like "Lucas is really good at sports" and leave it at that. The person(s) doing the team selection will know what you mean.

Here's another example: suppose there's a member of your extended family who is married to an immigrant named Ana.

Your family members often discuss Ana with disdain, in front of your child, by inferring she's a typically lazy immigrant. They express remorse for her husband who has to do all the work.

Tell your child the next time it happens, they could say something like *"We don't know if their household workload seems off-balance because of Ana's heritage. There are so many other possible reasons."*

Then suggest that your child could leave the room whenever the conversation is taking place to indicate again that they don't agree with their assumption about Ana.

Explain that they can be Ana's ally without actually being in her presence.

Provide as many words and action options as you can for responding to unfair scenarios. The goal is to allow your child to pick the one that feels right for them.

Work on what words to use, together. Make it a shared conversation.

Standing up for what's right without jeopardizing their own safety is a *really* important skill for kids to learn.

Chapter 4.
Household Adjustments

One of the more effective ways to guide your child toward DEI values is to create an inclusive environment at home by making smart household choices.

Children are heavily influenced by teachers and peers, that's true. But the most lasting values are most often taught at home.

Step 1. Set an Example

As you probably already know, children rarely buy the "Do as I say, not as I do" approach.

If you say something is important, but your child doesn't see you behaving in a way that matches your words, they know it's not actually that important to you, so why should it be important to them?

On the flip side, if they see you doing something that's aligned with what you've been telling them, your words will be much more effective.

Here are some ideas for setting an example so your child can fully embrace your guidance.

Be aware of your own biases. If you behave in ways that demonstrate you're skeptical about diversity and inclusion values, even though you say otherwise, your child will notice and emulate your behavior.

Learning for Justice explains "Studies show people can be consciously committed to egalitarianism, and deliberately work to behave without prejudice, yet still possess hidden negative prejudices or stereotypes. Implicit Association Tests (IATs) can tap those hidden, or automatic, stereotypes and prejudices that circumvent conscious control. Project Implicit—a collaborative research effort between researchers at Harvard University, the University of Virginia, and University of Washington—offers dozens of such tests."[5]

Call out discrimination. If someone says or does something against a specific group of people in your own home and you don't intervene or say something in the moment, that will signal to your child that you're okay with that type of language or behavior.

Speak kind words. Whenever someone shares something unique about themselves with you (and your child is listening), you could say things like, *"Wow, that is so interesting!"* or *"I didn't know that. I'm really glad you shared it with me."* The goal is to teach your child how to treat all different types of people with kindness and respect.

Show support for a work colleague or someone at your child's school. Make a stand if you see someone being teased. Silence and inaction in the face of injustice sends the message that it's okay to look the other way. Instead of ignoring the issue, write an editorial in your local newspaper, call your elected official, or talk to a manager. Just do something to be proactive.

Step 2. Promote DEI Values with Household Routines

Here are some ideas for shaping your home environment to reflect DEI values:

Media. Talking about acceptance is a good first step, but it's not enough. Select movies, videos, TV shows, etc. that depict all different types of people.Common Sense Media is a great resource for finding appropriate media.

HOW TO RAISE INCLUSIVE CHILDREN

Your media selection doesn't have to consistently include marginalized people, but it's important that it never includes uncontested discrimination.

This might sound like an impossible task at first, but if you can start getting your family into the habit of choosing media based on fairness and acceptance and not based on a world where it's okay to discriminate and be unkind, you'll be doing them an enormous favor. Try it.

Books. In addition to keeping an open dialogue about DEI values, another key to raising equality-minded children is to fill your family bookshelf with stories that include marginalized people (LGBTQ+, immigrants, etc.). Storylines that focus on the experience itself are fine, but storylines that include marginalized people as an integral part of the story are even better.

Friends. Friendships can be one of the richest, most authentic learning experiences for instilling DEI values. Sharing a meal with different types of people, going on adventures, inviting one another to special cultural events familiarizes them with *your* culture and exposes you to *their* culture. The goal here is to help children associate DEI values with the warm characteristics of friendship: human connection and kindness.

Food. Try to establish a family meal night that celebrates food from another country. To start, pick something that you think your kids might like. Then encourage them to suggest meals from other countries. Repeat the meals that are successful.

Art. Display art in your home that was created by someone from another culture. Place the artwork somewhere that's seen by the whole family every day. Talk about what it means to you.

Family mission statement. Things you say to your kids repeatedly (randomly) can have an enormous impact on how their opinions form as they grow. Keep saying things like "we believe in justice for *all* humans" or "everyone is different"—anything that denotes fairness and acceptance. Trust us, it will sink in eventually.

Family decisions. To promote the notion of democracy, allow your children a vote in family decision-making. Doing this provides a tangible experience of the democratic process, teaching them that their voice matters and contributes to collective outcomes.

Step 3. Make Household Conversations About DEI Values Ongoing

Teaching fairness for *all* humans is not a once-and-done conversation. Issues will come up all the time that your child (hopefully) feels comfortable sharing with you.

As any parent knows, getting a concept to sink in with kids needs to be repeated over and over again. Keep guiding them toward fairness and acceptance.

Children need constant help understanding why each situation is either fair or unfair. Basically, children are a work in progress.

Childhood education expert Carol McNulty confirms: "They have not yet reached the point of fully recognizing the needs of others." [6]

Conversations about DEI values need to be a work in progress too.

Talking about fairness and acceptance repeatedly might feel cumbersome to you, but it hopefully doesn't to your child. They're progressively applying what you tell them to scenarios in their own life and deciding if it makes sense or not.

HOW TO RAISE INCLUSIVE CHILDREN

Depending on their attention span, who knows when you will say or model the right words at the right time. Keep trying. Plan for a marathon, not a sprint.

Here's another tip: there will be times when they want to talk to you that aren't convenient—like when you're working, reading, or talking with someone else. Either make the time then or ask your child to remember their thoughts so they can share with you later.

The good news is that the decisions your kids make as they grow through adolescence and into early adulthood will be informed by your ongoing conversations and actions at home.

Chapter 5.
Find Out What Your Child Already Knows

It's so important for you to find out what your child already knows about diversity and inclusion. If you start guiding them by saying things they already know, they're likely to stop listening.

Maybe they're already well-versed in all aspects of current and past issues. Or maybe they know very little about DEI and you're starting with a blank slate. Or maybe their knowledge falls somewhere in the middle.

Regardless, you'll never know until you get them talking and really listen to their words.

Also, because kids tend to avoid face-to-face, formal discussions, the best way to learn their opinion is to listen and learn sporadically. There's no need for a one-time, sit-down, eye-to-eye conversation. Keep it casual.

Step 1. Prompt Your Child to Share Their Thoughts

The best way to get most children to open up is to say the minimum. If you use short phrases that reassure and prompt, you're more likely to get a response.

The goal here is to get your child to feel comfortable enough to express how they feel.

The other crucial element is timing. Trying to start a conversation while your child is playing, reading, watching TV or a video almost never works.

They'll probably find it intrusive before you even start talking. Plus, you won't have their full attention.

If it's not the right time, wait. As many parents know, timing is everything, especially when you're trying to discover a child's true feelings.

If it *is* a good time, here are some ideas for sparking a conversation.

Read a book together. Reading a book together is a great way to elicit your child's true feelings about a given subject.

There are lots and lots of wonderful children's books that tell engaging stories about all kinds of different human experiences and support the notion that *everyone* deserves kindness and respect.

Try to keep in mind though that many of these books might arouse feelings of sadness. If so, always help your child feel safe and loved.

If they have questions, take time to answer thoroughly. Steer the conversation away from sadness. Make kindness and respect your guiding principles.

Keep it casual. Keep your discovery tactics as nonchalant as possible. Kids are much more likely to respond honestly when they feel comfortable.

As you go about your lives together, gather clues here and there. This could be in the car, at the store, eating a meal, or watching TV together. Try to initiate informal conversations anywhere that seems appropriate to you - you know your child best.

HOW TO RAISE INCLUSIVE CHILDREN

Resources for Early Learning explains "Conversation helps children express their thoughts, get what they need, resolve conflicts, ask for help, and learn from adults and from one another." [7]

Current events. The daily news, often filled with social, political, and environmental issues, presents invaluable opportunities for meaningful parent-child conversations.

Instead of shielding your child from these realities, engaging with them in an age-appropriate manner can foster critical thinking, empathy, and a deeper understanding of the world beyond their immediate experience.

Here's an example:

Stories about poverty seem to be appearing more and more frequently. Hopefully mentioning one of the (age-appropriate) subjects below will prompt a reaction:

- **Kids who don't have toys**
- **Kids who have to work instead of going to school**
- **Homeless people with pets**

If your child perks up when you mention any of the subjects above or something else, offer to explore further together. A simple online search should enable you *both* to learn more.

If they're not interested in learning more, leave it alone for now and bring up the subject again later.

These conversations about current events not only enhance your child's sense of social responsibility but can also strengthen your mutual bond through shared learning and understanding of the world around them

Note: This is a perfect example of when a parent knows best what is and isn't appropriate for their own child's level of development. Tread lightly here—current events can be hard to handle (even for adults).

Dig deep. Regardless of the subject of your casual conversation, it's important to read between the lines of what they're telling you or asking you.

For example, suppose your child tells you that one of their classmates, Gabriella, hasn't been in school for two weeks.

Before you react, find out more so you know what to say. Maybe it has nothing to do with immigration policies.

Ask what the teacher did when Gabriella missed school. What are your child's friends saying? Are they worried about Gabriella?

Your job is to discover how your child truly feels about Gabriella's disappearance. Maybe it really *is* about Gabriella's family's immigration status.

If so, continue subtly encouraging your child to contribute ideas so they feel like they're an important part of the discussion, which their generation absolutely is!

If your child doesn't respond to anything, save it for later. It might be that they've never even thought about immigration before.

Give them time to think about it. Keep trying until they're ready to share.

Try to remember that the whole point of this step is to get your child to talk so you can get an accurate understanding of how they truly feel about a given DEI subject.

Step 2. Listen Carefully

Once your child starts talking, listen attentively and silently. The only words you need to utter, if any, are to let them know you're eager to learn more. Be ready to listen without judgement.

Kids can tell if you're paying attention to them. An article in *Today's Parent* explains:

In Today's Parent, Claire Gagne confirms "When you're really connected, your body is leaning in, and your phone is down. You'll find that if you do a really good job in those moments, they will come to you for the hard stuff."[8]

Let your child sort through their feelings as they talk. Try to remember that this is not about you.

Say the minimum. While they're talking, if you feel like you're going to burst if you don't say something, feel free to nod your head and say, "hmmm."

Let them know you're interested. Here are some phrases you could use to let them know you're interested in what they're saying, and you want to learn more:

- *"Tell me more."*

- *"Wow, you have quite a story to share."*

- *"Please keep talking. I'm really interested."*

- *"It sounds like you have a lot on your mind, so I'm glad you're sharing."*

- *"I love that you're so open and honest with your feelings."*

- *"It means a lot to me that you feel comfortable talking to me."*

- *"You're doing a great job of describing what happened."*

- *"Could you repeat that? I want to be sure I understand what you're going through."*

Step 3. Stay Impartial

Even if what your child is saying is completely against everything you believe, try to remind yourself that this is their time to talk and your time to listen and learn.

They need to know that you're truly listening to their words.

Neutral Zone. Remember, it's important to keep your discovery tactics and opinions to yourself. Otherwise, you run the risk of making them feel like you're making moral judgements about what they're telling you. The very last thing you want to do is create a barrier for any future meaningful back-and-forth discussions.

Unexpected Opportunities. Sometimes opportunities arise unexpectedly that are perfect for learning your child's true opinion. For example, maybe on TV, there's a show about a transgender person and your brother, Uncle Don to your kids, says something derogatory.

Follow up with your child later and ask them, "What did you think about Uncle Don's statement about transgender people when we were watching TV?"

Starting a conversation about Uncle Don's opinion can create an open space for discussion. A scenario like this could potentially give you enormous insight into how your child really feels about the subject.

Again, learning your child's true opinion requires active listening.

The Center for Parenting Education tells us: "By listening to them, you are communicating that they are worthy of your attention." [9]

One day your child will hopefully follow your lead and really listen to whomever they're with.

TRISH ALLISON

Section II.
Individual DEI Subjects

In Section I, we discussed the fundamentals of DEI communication with kids. Now it's time to get into individual DEI subjects.

Each of the following chapters addresses a standalone topic, such as immigration, transgender, poverty, and disabilities, along with suggested strategies for engaging with your child about the subject and how to guide them.

The following chapters can be read in any order.

Chapter 6.
Immigration

Kids don't usually need (or want) to know details about the politics behind immigration policies. Nor do they need to know the difference between asylum and naturalized citizenship.

Instead, the approach here is to provide answers to basic questions, such as *what is an immigrant?* and *why do immigrants leave their home country?*

When you feel like your child understands immigration basics, you can connect your discussion to the real world by talking about your own family's heritage.

Strive to be as reassuring as possible. Make sure you're using age-appropriate language that makes them feel safe. If they look worried, pivot the conversation to something more optimistic.

Step 1. Start with the Basics

What is an immigrant?

Explain that an immigrant is a person living in a country other than that of his or her birth. An immigrant can be an adult or a child.

An immigrant can even be a plant or an animal. For example, a bear found in Alaska that has previously only been found in Montana is called an immigrant bear.

This is a good time to ask your child if they know any immigrants. If they're not 100% sure, offer your own ideas.

If you know someone who is an immigrant, talk about their situation. Have they been in their new country a long time? Do they have kids who attend school? How well do you know them? Are they good people? Are they worried about being deported?

Offer as many words of encouragement as you can here. It's best to begin your child's understanding of immigrants with a sense of confidence.

The odds of them wanting to learn more will be much greater if they feel confident about the subject from the beginning.

Why do immigrants leave their home country?

Clarify that there are many reasons why immigrants leave their home country.

Sometimes they're fleeing because they fear for their safety. Sometimes they can't find work in their home country. Sometimes it's because a family member is already in the new country.

Or maybe they need better healthcare, or their homeland was destroyed by a natural disaster.

Regardless of the reason, immigrants are most often seeking a better life for themselves and for their families. It's a hard decision for them to leave their home. Their journey is often long and arduous.

If you feel like your child is emotionally ready, ask them to imagine what it would feel like if they were told they were going on a long one-way trip and could only take a few of their favorite toys (and clothes) with them.

This will hopefully connect the plight of immigrant families with your child's world. Talk about it together. Make sure they feel safe.

HOW TO RAISE INCLUSIVE CHILDREN

Talk about your own family's heritage

To help your child feel more connected to the subject of immigration, it's important to help them understand their own family's heritage. When you broach the subject, it makes them feel like you're sharing special information with them.

The goal is to help them feel pride in their own heritage first so they can then relate that feeling to immigrants.

In an article aptly titled "Why It's Important to Teach Your Kids About Genealogy," we learn "Knowing your lineage and feeling connected to your family is always advantageous, but when you start learning as a kid the benefits seem to multiply." [10]

Kids love to learn about their family's past, and the benefits are enormous. Look online together to discover where your family's ancestors originated.

Talk about it. Make it fun. Does your family have any rituals related to your heritage? Traditional ones? New ones?

Help your child develop a sense of pride in their heritage and your family's country of origin.

Then mention that other families most likely also have their own traditions that give them a warm feeling when they experience their traditions together.

Learning about your ancestors, celebrating family traditions, embracing your culture, and understanding where you came from can really help your child make a mental connection between their own sense of belonging and the plight of immigrants.

As you're discovering and discussing your family tree together, keep in mind that the goal is to help your child feel empathy and respect for immigrants.

Step 2. Explain What Happens When Immigrants Arrive in a New Country

It's time to help your child understand how challenging it can be for immigrants to move to a new country—not just the journey itself, but the endless backlash and adjustments they need to make once they arrive.

But be careful not to make it sound too scary. Try to spin this information into a "positive" discussion. One way to do that is to emphasize that immigrants need allies to help them feel like they belong.

Talk about the immigrant journey

Start by explaining that immigrants usually arrive at the border of their new country after a long and perilous journey.

Immigrants make the journey by foot, train, horseback, plane, boat, or all of the above. Typically, they spend days, weeks, months, or sometimes even years getting to their destination. Often, they're delayed by imprisonment in jails and detention centers.

Sometimes, one member of an immigrant family journeys to a new country on their own leaving the rest of their family behind. The reason for this independent migration is most often because one member of the family feels a duty to forge ahead and find safety before endangering the rest of the family.

Try to keep in mind that the goal here isn't to scare your child, but simply to give them a sense of how strongly immigrants want and need to improve their lives by moving to a new country.

Instead of getting into gory details about the journey itself, you can base your discussion on immigrants' willingness to endure a dangerous journey as a testament to their determination to seek out a better future.

If your child looks worried as you're talking, reassure them that not all countries treat immigrants unfairly once they arrive.

Some countries actually help immigrants adjust to their new world. You could say something similar to what's recommended in an article titled "How to Talk to Your Child About Immigration":

"There are also many people that want to help and welcome immigrants. We want everyone to belong and feel safe here. If you ever feel unsafe or if someone says something that is not nice, you can tell me." [11]

Reassure them that if they ever feel worried or unsafe, they can always come to you.

Explain the impact of cultural differences

The immigrants who do make it to their new country often speak a different language, making their daily lives especially hard.

Other cultural differences that immigrants experience include new holidays, different food, and distinctive music. Everything is unfamiliar to them.

Here are some ideas for explaining cultural differences at a kid's level.

Holidays. Holiday celebrations are the best way to explain immigrants' cultural differences to kids. Tell your child that the two holidays that are celebrated by most people around the world are Christmas and New Year's Day. The rest of the holidays are unique to each country's culture. For example, no other country besides the U.S. celebrates the 4th of July.

Language. To explain the language barrier, you could say something like *"Think about how frustrating and scary it is to listen to a group of people talking in a language you've never heard before. Now flip that. Try to imagine how scary and frustrating it must be for an immigrant to be surrounded, daily, by people speaking in a language they don't know."* This is a perfect opportunity for your child to feel a sense of empathy for the immigrant plight.

Food. Holiday meals are another great way to explain the difference between immigrants and their host countries to kids. For example, most immigrants who come to America have never even heard of Thanksgiving. Eating turkey and stuffing on a specific Thursday in November is completely new to them. Same with hot dogs on July 4th, or ham on Easter Sunday, or eggnog at Christmas—all Americanized food traditions.

Music. Most countries in the world have their own distinct musical tastes. Some examples are Scottish bagpipes, Latin salsa, German polka music, or Jamaican reggae. But when immigrants arrive in a new country, they typically have to actively seek out music from their home country because it's not often found on local radio stations.

Always try to put a positive spin on anything about immigrants that you communicate to your child. For example, when talking about cultural differences you could say something like:

HOW TO RAISE INCLUSIVE CHILDREN

"Even though getting used to a new culture is a complicated subject for immigrants, the ideas and customs that they bring with them can forever enrich the new country.

For example, immigrants have made so many positive contributions to American food culture, such as pizza and tacos. We'd never even know about those foods if it weren't for Italian and Mexican immigrants!"

Answer questions about immigrants' daily anxiety

Continue explaining the extreme difficulties that immigrants face by answering your child's questions.

Even though kids sometimes ask pointed questions that are hard to answer, it's important for them to know that you're listening and interested in responding to their curiosity.

"Avoiding a child's question does not make the question go away. Instead, not being able to talk about a situation can make children more scared and more worried."[11]

Instead of avoiding questions, try to find that sweet spot between accurately depicting immigrants' struggles and making sure your child feels safe.

For example, if your child asks a question like, *"Why do kids get separated from their parents?"*, your answer could be, *"That will never happen to our family. If you're concerned though, I'm here to answer your questions anytime."*

Make sure your child feels comforted before continuing with your response.

"If immigrants want to stay in a new country that's different from their country of origin, they must go through a years-long process to gain citizenship. Until then, they live in constant anxiety and fear that they could be deported.

Raids are common. The purpose of raids is to round up immigrants who are in their new country illegally.

The level of stress about raids can be overwhelming. So overwhelming in fact that it's common for immigrants to suffer from chronic mental health problems, which of course decreases their chance of staying in a new country."

Again, check in with your child to make sure they feel safe.

Explain why immigrants need allies

It's time to infuse some optimism into this subject.

The good news is that immigrants need allies. They need someone who can help them participate in their new culture and help them feel like they belong.

Talk about how much of a difference in someone's life an ally can make. Especially since immigration has become such a charged political issue, your child can really make a difference by befriending an immigrant.

The goal here is simply to help your child feel special because they have a real chance to make someone's life feel less lonely. Simultaneously, this is also a great opportunity for them to learn first-hand the positive effects of kindness.

HOW TO RAISE INCLUSIVE CHILDREN

Note to reader: We're fully aware of the current situation surrounding U.S. immigrant deportation policies. But instead of dwelling on sadness and fear, we opted to provide suggestions for parents to help their children develop enduring, *positive* feelings toward immigrants.

What you don't want is for your child to carry negative feelings about immigrants into adulthood. Try to remember that the current political climate is *temporary*.

That said, helping your child feel safe is a priority. If your child asks you a question about immigration, answer them in a way that is both age-appropriate and also helps them feel safe.

For example, you could say something like *"Some people are not being nice to immigrants. But there are also many people who want to welcome and help immigrants. Everyone should feel safe. You can absolutely come to me anytime if you ever feel unsafe or if someone says something hurtful."*

TRISH ALLISON

Chapter 7.
Transgender

First, this chapter is not about helping your child understand their own gender. Rather, it's about helping you proactively and intermittently teach them that transgender people deserve the same kindness and respect as everyone else.

Like the rest of the subjects in this book, transgender acceptance has ebbs and flows. We're currently in a temporary ebb, unfortunately. And we won't be able to enjoy further, sustainable movement in the right direction until we can provide accurate information to the upcoming generation.

That doesn't mean you have to become an expert on the transgender subject. But it *does* mean teaching your kid(s) that it is a fundamental human right that everyone has the right to dress, act, and identify in ways that make them feel good about themselves.

While there's no one-size-fits-all approach for teaching kids understanding and respect for transgender people, this chapter provides practical suggestions for scenarios that you can tailor to fit your own situation.

Step 1. Start with the Basics

Explain what a transgender person is

The best way to explain transgender to kids is to keep it simple. All they need to know is that your brain is telling you one thing, but your body parts don't match what your brain is telling you.

It's not a flaw; it's just a cell-growth mix-up that can happen at birth to anyone.

Here's a simple definition: Transgender people's inner thoughts don't match their outside parts. For example, maybe someone constantly has thoughts like, "Wow that dress is really pretty. I wish I could wear it."

But that person has a penis so everyone assumes they're a boy and shouldn't wear dresses.

The most important thing for your child to learn about transgender people is that they're exactly the same as everyone else, except for this one part of how their gender works.

You can remind them that *everyone* is born with traits that make them different from other people—not just transgender people.

Here are some words you could consider sharing to make your point:

"We're all different from each other. We should always accept people for how they are and make sure they feel safe and

included. It's never okay to make people feel sad or left out just because they're different."

Offer as many words of encouragement as you can here. It's best to begin your child's understanding of transgender with a sense of confidence.

The odds of them wanting to learn more will be much greater if they feel confident enough to participate in a mutual conversation.

A new study from the Journal of Neuroscience indicates that back-and-forth conversations with kids are not only beneficial to their confidence but also to their brain development.

"...conversational turns are associated with more coherent white-matter connectivity and indicates that promoting such conversational turns may enhance structural brain development and the language abilities supported by that brain development in children from all backgrounds. [12]

As you're reviewing the basics with your child, keep in mind that they need verbal confirmation that it's okay to ask you questions anytime.

Make sure they know you can talk about it together. Reiterate your message as many times as needed.

Talk about the basics of the transgender transition process

Just like you did in the previous step, keep it simple. You don't want your child to feel like you're talking down to them.

Here are some simple words you could consider using to define the transgender transition process:

"Transitioning is the process of changing the way you look on the outside, so it matches the way you feel on the inside. It can involve medical treatment and hormones, or it can involve changing your name and preferred pronouns, or both. There are lots of different options, but the final decision is always up to the individual."

If you can relate your definition to someone you know personally, it will help your child process what you're saying.

For example, if you know someone who is transgender, talk about their situation. Have they already had reassignment hormone therapy? Did they have any surgery? What has it been like for them to embrace their gender identity?

If you don't know a transgender person, do an online search. Try to find someone you think your child might be familiar with.

It's important that they're able to connect transgender with a real person. Having a visual representation will help them understand the basics of transitioning.

Your child will inevitably have follow-up questions/concerns. It's crucial for them to feel like they have a safe, informed, reliable adult they can confide in about anything, anytime. Your response is an indication of whether they can count on you to talk when they need you.

Also, be consistent with your answers. This will allow them to better understand the issues and build empathy and compassion. The goal!

Step 2. Learn How to Answer Kids' Questions About Transgender People

While the questions and suggested simple answers below are by no means exhaustive, they'll hopefully provide a good starting point for responding to the inevitable awkward questions and statements that most kids come up with about transgender people.

Q: What does transgender mean?

A: "A transgender person feels one way in their brain but that feeling doesn't match their outside parts."

Q: Is transgender a mental illness?

A: "No. It's not considered a mental illness."

Q: What's transphobia?

A: "Transphobia is fear and hatred of transgender people."

Q: What is cisgender?

A: *"Cisgender means that your outside parts match the gender you identify with inside yourself."*

Q: Do all transgender people have surgery?

A: *"No. There are many reasons, but the most common one is cost."*

Q: Can men have babies?

A: *"A person who was born female and is living as a male can have a baby if their female organs are still fully productive."*

Q: Have transgender people always existed?

A: *"Yes, transgender people have always existed. But whether or not they're recognized and/or accepted varies from culture to culture."*

Q: Is being transgender like playing dress-up?

A: *"No, it's not just playing. For transgender people, their gender identity—who they know they are inside—is real and important to them. It's not about pretending."*

Q: Is being transgender a choice?

A: *"No, being transgender isn't a choice. It's how some people are born. Just like you don't choose to be a boy or a girl, transgender people don't choose to be transgender."*

Q: Do all transgender people take medicine?

A: *"Some transgender people take medicine called hormones to help their bodies change, but not all of them do. Again,* it's a personal choice, and it doesn't define whether someone is transgender."

Q: What if I accidentally use the wrong pronoun?

A: "It's okay! Just say a quick 'Sorry,' and then use the correct pronoun. Everyone makes mistakes sometimes, and it's important to try your best."

Q: Can transgender people be my friend?

A: "Absolutely! Being transgender is just one part of who a person is. They can be kind, funny, smart, and have all sorts of great qualities, just like anyone else."

Q: How does someone know that they're transgender?

A: "Most often, transgender people have vague feelings of not fitting in for a long time. It's completely up to the individual whether they act on those feelings by recognizing their own gender identity."

Q: Can transgender people use the same bathroom?

A: "Yes. Transgender girls are girls, and transgender boys are boys. They should be able to use the bathroom that matches how they live as a boy or a girl."

Q: Have I met a transgender person before and not known it?

A: "It's possible! Transgender people are just like other people, and you might not always know someone is transgender unless they tell you."

Q: What's the difference between being transgender and being gay?

A: "Being transgender is about your gender identity, who you are inside, like being a boy or a girl. A transgender person can like boys, girls, both, or neither, just like anyone else. Being gay (or lesbian) is about who you like, who you have feelings for."

Society's understanding of transgender is continually evolving. There might be times when your child is asking you questions, and you feel awkward because you don't know the answer.

Looking online for the answer is perfectly fine. Just be sure to involve your child.

This is a great opportunity to engage your child in the process of learning. You'll be showing them what it means to be open and curious.

Follow up

Many questions about transgender people can and should come up as your child weaves their way through life. Let them know, repeatedly, that they can come to you anytime.

Try to continue bringing up the subject as the weeks and months unfold after your child asks a question. Teaching respect for transgender people is not a formal, once-and-done conversation. Encourage your child to keep asking questions.

HOW TO RAISE INCLUSIVE CHILDREN

Remember that the values you teach your child will be much more impactful if your discussions are casual, consistent, and intermittent.

TRISH ALLISON

Chapter 8.
Poverty

The first time your child becomes aware of poverty could be when they see a homeless person on the street. Or maybe they have a friend who consistently wears the same tattered clothes every day.

As heartbreaking as these visions can be for a young person, it's our job as adults to help them understand that humans are more than their financial circumstances.

As children witness poverty and look for answers, the goal is to help them get their answers from someone they love and trust. You!

The good news is that you don't have to become an expert in socioeconomics to guide kids toward understanding the realities of poverty. Most kids don't need (or want) complicated details.

But it is important to help them understand that the majority of poor people's lives have devolved as a result of circumstances that are completely out of their control. It's not because they made bad choices.

Yes, it can be a scary topic, but kids need to know that poor people didn't do anything wrong and therefore deserve the same kindness and respect as everyone else.

Bright Horizons confirms this sentiment in the article "Talking with Children About Poverty and Homelessness," "As parents, we want to protect our children from the more frightening aspects of life, including homelessness and poverty. But children see more than we think they do—and like so many complicated issues, we want them to get their information from us, not TV or their friends.

Importantly, children have an innate desire to help others and are interested in social issues. We can foster this natural tendency and channel it into action by having open, honest, intentional conversations about the issues of poverty and homelessness." [13]

Remember that your job is to subtly integrate a realistic understanding of poor people into the (casual) conversations and activities you share with your children as they grow.

Try to talk about poverty intermittently instead of abruptly starting one long formal conversation. If you try to talk about it all at once, you run the risk that they'll stop listening every time you bring up the subject.

In addition to keeping your explanations sporadic, try to keep them as non-threatening as possible. It's important to explain the truth about poverty *without* triggering tears.

As you're talking, consider your child's age and developmental ability and try to find a balance between explaining reality and sharing distressing details.

Step 1. Start with the Basics

Define poverty using simple terms

Start by offering a simple definition of poverty. There's no need to include graphic details of starving children or lengthy explanations about the political greed that prevents someone from earning a livable wage.

Keep your *initial* (casual!) discussion simple. It's important for kids to feel confident about the subject so they fully believe in their ability to participate in any further discussion.

HOW TO RAISE INCLUSIVE CHILDREN

You could say something simple like:

> *"Poverty means not having enough money for basic needs like food, shelter, and clothing."*

Pause after you say this. It will hopefully give you a chance to see if your child is truly tuned into the conversation.

If you don't get any reaction at all, save the conversation for another time. But if your child *does* look interested in learning more, your next job is to engage them in the discussion.

First offer an example from *your* world about someone you know who's poor. Maybe there's someone you know who lives a very meager existence. Talk about their clothes, transportation, food, entertainment, etc.

Whatever example from your own world that you can share is a great way to start things off. If you can think of someone you *both* know, even better, because it gives your child a visual image for the discussion.

Ask your child if *they* know anyone who might be poor. You could ask follow-up leading questions about that person. Why does your child think that person is poor? Where do they live? What do they eat?

Then depending on their maturity level, you could talk about the "working poor."

In our present-day society, it's harder than ever to make ends meet. Some people who have jobs and work hard seven days a week earn incomes that still fall below the poverty line.

Worse, the official measure of the working poor continues to slide downward. It now includes well-educated people who work hard but still have to live a life filled with perpetual stress about not having enough money.

Tread lightly here though. If your child is sensitive to topics like this and feels overwhelmed by their emotions, you could be risking that they'll shut down permanently every time someone brings up the subject of poverty.

If your child seems overwhelmed, pause the conversation and pick it up another time. This is really important.

Remember the point of this chapter is *not* to make children feel bad about their own situation. Instead, the point is to help them understand that just because someone is poor, doesn't mean it's their fault or that they deserve less respect than anyone else.

Talk about homelessness

One of the most important concepts to get across in this step is that being homeless doesn't make you a bad person.

When you're together and you cross paths with a homeless person whether it's on the sidewalk or in the car, ask your child if they noticed the person. Then proactively express your feelings about the situation. You could say something like:

"I think it's sad that a person doesn't have anywhere to live."

or

"Even though that person looks angry, they're still a human being who deserves to be treated with kindness and respect."

Whatever you choose to say, say *something*. It's so important not to shy away from subjects like this. If you do, you risk sending the message that you're indifferent to people in need, and that's what your child will pick up from the situation.

Offer to help using whatever gesture your family is comfortable with.

> *Additionally, in "Talking to Kids About Homelessness," we learn "Kids' questions about a homeless person usually stem from genuine curiosity. That person doesn't fall into any of the categories of people with whom they're familiar. They're not passing judgment; just wondering. The young child's initial impression is heavily influenced by the parent's affect, actions, and responses to his questions. And it is by observation of the parent that the child first gets his cues about how to react and feel. So, as you answer your child's questions, be aware of the attitude you may be projecting."*[14]

Once you see that your child is curious, that's your cue to react to the situation and start the conversation.

Another crucial concept to communicate is that people are homeless for lots of different reasons. It's not due to individual failure.

For example, maybe that person got injured or sick and couldn't afford to pay for a doctor. Or maybe they lost their job and couldn't find another one. Usually, it's a combination of things that force people to leave their homes.

Regardless of the reason, the point to make here is that it's not the fault of the homeless person that they're in such an unfortunate situation. It's not because they're too lazy or too dumb to get a job.

Also, don't forget about body language. If you walk briskly past a homeless person and avoid making eye contact, your child might assume poor people are scary.

Every homeless person has an individual story about what they've been through and how they got there. The goal is to encourage compassion, not judgement.

Dissuade any thinking you detect that your child is considering homeless people as a group that needs to be blamed.

> "Sometimes parents try to use homeless people as an example of what could happen to the child if he or she doesn't stay in school or doesn't go to college or engages in risky behavior." The Huffington Post article goes on to explain, "This is a bad idea, and it is generally not true. You want to use the situation to cultivate feelings of empathy and action, not shaming."[15]

Here's another idea for bringing humanity into the equation. Try to steer the conversation toward helping your child think about what homeless people might be feeling instead of just an object to be talked about.

The feelings you talk about can be simple: hungry? scared? cold? lonely?

Your child will inevitably (hopefully) have follow-up questions/concerns. It's crucial for them to feel like they have a safe, informed, reliable adult they can confide in about anything, anytime.

Remember to be consistent with your answers. This will allow them to better understand homelessness and build empathy and compassion. The goal!

Encourage volunteering

Volunteering your time and/or gently used items is a great way to get the "help less fortunate people" wheels turning in your child's head.

HOW TO RAISE INCLUSIVE CHILDREN

Take them with you to a local shelter to serve a meal or have them participate with you in a coat-giving drive.

Be sure to explain (briefly!) who you're helping and why. Kids can tune out quickly when adults are talking—try to keep your explanations short.

Ask them to help you load the coats you're donating into your car. The act of *physically* gathering items to donate creates a more memorable impression than just talking about it.

Hopefully, helping *you* will motivate your child to help those who are less fortunate, on their own. Maybe they'll even feel inspired to organize their own donation event.

Think about it. They'll have to figure out where to get items to be donated, where to store them, how to organize them, which items should go to whom, etc.

Be sure to offer help when needed, e.g., driving, searching online for donation addresses, etc. And of course, remember to praise them for being so kind.

This type of brain activity helps kids feel like they're tactically controlling an outcome (a.k.a. making a difference). It can be incredibly helpful for teaching kids how good it feels to help others.

Here are more ideas for encouraging volunteerism:

- Suggest they pull outgrown clothes from their closet to donate to a shelter. Encourage them by giving them something to put their outgrown clothes in.
- Offer the option of doing an extra chore to earn a "pay it forward" allowance, so they have money of their own to donate to a charity. Help them research a charity where they

could donate their allowance money.
- During winter holidays, for every new toy they receive, suggest that your child can pick one of their own older toys to give to a family in need.
- Run a sock drive. For their birthday, suggest that they ask for a pair of new socks to be donated with their gift.
- Ask for *their* ideas. You could say something like, "*What do you think we could do to help?*"

Offer reassurance

Talking about poverty and homelessness might cause your child to feel anxious that your family might run out of food or be homeless someday.

If you have a friend or relative who might help you if things get bleak, you could say something like, *"We could always live with grandma if we didn't have our own home, but that will never happen."*

Remind your child that regardless of your family's circumstances, you'll always figure out how to endure *together*. They'll never be alone; you'll always keep them safe.

Sharing anything beyond that could possibly be too much for them to handle.

Step 2. Learn How to Answer Kids' Questions About Poverty and Homelessness

While the questions and suggested simple answers below are by no means exhaustive, they'll hopefully provide a good starting point for responding to the inevitable awkward questions that most kids come up with.

HOW TO RAISE INCLUSIVE CHILDREN

Try to remember to keep your answers simple.

Q: Why does Lydia wear the same dress every day?

A: "That might be her only dress. Or maybe it's her favorite dress. We don't know the full story."

Q: How come that woman is asking strangers for money?

A: "She probably needs money to buy food because she's hungry."

Q: Why don't they have a place to live?

A: "That's a good question. I don't know for sure. Sometimes it's because a person doesn't have the money to pay for a house or an apartment."

Q: What if we lose our house?

A: "We'll always be able to provide a home for our family. But if we did ever lose our home, and again it's not likely, we could move in with grandma and grandpa, find an apartment, or go to a temporary shelter."

Q: Why are they acting like that?

A: "Some kinds of illnesses affect the way a person thinks or acts. People with special training can sometimes help those people."

Q: Why isn't that man wearing any shoes?

A: "His old shoes probably wore out, and he can't afford to buy new ones."

Q: Why don't all homeless people stay in shelters?

A: "Sometimes there isn't enough room in the shelter to help everyone, or there's a limit on the amount of time you can stay in a shelter. Or maybe it's because of a personal reason. There are lots of different reasons."

Q: Why is that person pushing a shopping cart full of belongings?

A: *"Most likely because they don't have a home to put their stuff in, and they need a way to carry it around."*

Q: Why won't you give that person any money?

A: *"I don't usually give poor people money because I prefer to buy them food. Let's go into that bagel shop and buy some food for them."*

There might be times when your child asks a question, and you feel awkward because you don't know the answer.

Turning to the internet for the answer is perfectly fine. Just be sure to involve your child. This is a great opportunity to engage your child in the process of learning.

You'll be showing them what it means to be curious and willing to learn. Learning about other people is part of wanting to make the world a better place.

Follow up

Many questions about poverty will most likely come up as your child weaves their way through life. Let them know, repeatedly, that they can come to you anytime.

Try to continue bringing up the subject as the weeks and months unfold after your child asks a question. Teaching kids about poverty is not a formal, once-and-done conversation. Encourage your child to keep asking questions.

Remember to keep your discussions casual, consistent, and simple.

HOW TO RAISE INCLUSIVE CHILDREN

Chapter 9.
LGBTQ+

Note: Before you start discussing LGBTQ+ equality, make sure your child knows this is not a "birds and bees" sex talk—otherwise, you run the risk of them shutting down (from embarrassment) before the discussion even begins.

As a parent/caregiver, you have the power to ensure that your child learns sustainable norms and habits that encourage equality for all. But like anything of value, it takes time for seeds to grow.

> *In the article, "Role of Parents in Inculcating Values," we learn "It takes time to acquire a habit, and parents need to be patient with their children. Keep repeating these habits every day so the child inculcates it more promptly. Sometimes, parents are not aware what habits they should teach their children."*[16]

This chapter fills that parenting need by providing practical tips that teach children long-term LGBTQ+ equality habits.

Each step/section is intentionally structured progressively to help you guide your child toward fully understanding that regardless of whom you love, *all* people deserve the same respect, kindness, and opportunities for success.

Step 1. Start Early with the Basics

It's never too early to help children understand that the gender of the person you love has no bearing on your integrity or your ability to have a healthy relationship.

> *The award-winning Reverend Dr. Jennifer Harvey states: "As early as age five, children recognize that different groups are treated differently."[17]*

Starting your discussions while they're young has the added benefit of laying the groundwork for more complicated discussions as they grow.

Additionally, there's no need yet to get into complicated subjects like persistent homophobia or how religion and homosexuality intersect.

Instead, keep it simple by limiting your discussion to a definition of the LGBTQ+ acronym.

The biggest advantage of keeping it simple at the beginning is that you're boosting your child's confidence. It's important for them to feel confident so that they believe in their ability to participate in the discussion.

A new study featured in *Reuters Health* indicates that back-and-forth conversations with kids are not only beneficial to their confidence but also to their brain development.

> *"These 'conversational turns' are strongly related to the physical strength of white-matter connections between the two key language regions in the left hemisphere of the brain."[18]*

As you're reviewing the basics *with* your child, keep in mind that they need *verbal* confirmation that it's okay to ask you questions anytime.

According to the book, *Raising White Kids: Bringing up Children in a Racially Unjust America,* your response should be *"an indication of whether they can count on you to talk when they need you."* [17]

HOW TO RAISE INCLUSIVE CHILDREN

Define the LGBTQ.+ acronym

Like all words and concepts that kids are curious about, it's best to confront their curiosity head-on and explain it simply and honestly so they don't assume a definition that they heard randomly.

One of the terms that seems to spark endless curiosity is the acronym "LGBTQ+." Tell your child you're happy to define the true meaning.

> *According to the article "Defining LGBTQ+ Words for Children," "When children ask questions about LGBTQ+ words, it is often best to offer simple and direct answers."[19]*

Here are some simple definitions:

- L is for "lesbian," which is romantic love between two women

- G is for "gay," which is romantic love between two men

- B is for "bisexual," which is when someone has romantic love for both men and women

- T is for "transgender," which is when someone shifts from one gender to another. (Note: If your child looks like they need more information here, you could say something like *"a transgender person's brain tells them something different from what their body parts define. For example, someone's inner thoughts might be something like 'That dress would look really good on me' but they have a penis so, according to society, they're not supposed to wear dresses."* If your child doesn't look curious, leave it alone.)

- Q is for "questioning," which is when someone understands that they are not heterosexual.

- \+ includes all other sexual orientations and gender identities.

Note: Depending on their age, you might want to remove the word "sex" from your definitions. For example, "transexual" could be "trans" and "heterosexual" could be "hetero."

Be sure to state that all these definitions are about love, how people find love in the world, and how people love themselves for who they are.

Encourage questions! If you don't know the answer, either figure it out together or tell them it's a great question and you need a little more time to think about a good answer.

Step 2. Learn How to Respond to LGBTQ+ Questions from Kids

LGBTQ+ issues in particular seem to spark lots of awkward questions from curious young minds. A smart general rule for answering these questions is to keep your answer simple and to focus on love and family.

While the questions, comments, and suggested simple answers below are by no means exhaustive, they'll hopefully provide a good starting point for responding to the inevitable awkward questions and statements that most kids come up with.

Often, children use the word *gay* to refer to someone who doesn't seem to fit in with other kids on the playground. The person who said it might not have actually meant their comment to be hurtful.

HOW TO RAISE INCLUSIVE CHILDREN

However, it's wrong and your child needs to know what the true definition of gay is, so they understand why it's wrong to use the word negatively.

The best solution here is to demystify the word *gay* by clarifying what it really means.

Explain that gay means there is a special love between two men. Continue by saying there's nothing wrong with gay love. The word *gay* should never be used in a negative way.

Leave it at that. You don't need to find out who said it or why. Let your child take the information you provided and apply it to their world at their own pace.

Here are our suggestions for answering common LGBTQ+ questions kids ask:

Q: Grandma says it's bad to have two moms. Is that true?

*A: "That's a common opinion in grandma's generation. LGBTQ inclusion in mainstream society wasn't accepted until recently. That's why previous generations, including grandma's, are still skeptical. The most important thing for you to remember is that we respect **all** families that love and care for their children."*

Q: Are LQBTQ family's real families?

> ***Note:*** *Any or all or a combination of the potential responses below are appropriate answers to this question.*

A: "Yes, LGBTQ families are real families."

"Every family is different. Some have different cultural traditions, religions, and values. Some have different structures—one parent instead of two, grandparents instead of parents, or two moms or two dads."

*"Despite any differences, **all** families deserve respect. Just because a family might look different from ours, doesn't mean they don't love each other just as much as we love each other."*

Q: How is it possible for two men to have a baby? Don't you need a man and a woman?

A: *"There are many different ways to become a parent. Some people get help from someone else to have a baby. Other people adopt babies. And sometimes two men raise children together because one of them was married to a woman before and had children with her."*

Q: Can animals be gay?

A: *"Yes, animals can be gay. Some animals are attracted to others of the same sex. For example, rams, penguins, and Japanese monkeys can be gay."*

Q: Why do gay and lesbian people have rainbow flags or rainbow stickers? What does it mean?

A: *"The rainbow flag and stickers represent support for the LGBTQ+ community. Anyone can use them to show support—you don't have to be gay to show support."*

Q: What's a *dyke*?

A: *"The word* dyke *is a negative term that's used to describe a lesbian. It's often used when someone is trying to be mean. Sometimes people use the word* dyke *to insult a girl who acts tough or to describe two girls who like each other a lot. It's not okay to use this word. It hurts people's feelings."*

Q: If girls play sports or if boys play with dolls, does that mean they're gay?

A: *"No, it doesn't mean they're gay. Some girls enjoy sports and competition. Some boys like to play with dolls."*

HOW TO RAISE INCLUSIVE CHILDREN

Q: Do gay men and lesbians have kids?

A: "Yes, many members of the LGBTQ community have children."

Q: Will I be gay if I play with someone who has two moms or two dads?

A: "No. You'll always be **you**, no matter whom you play with. Being gay or straight is something that's inside you. No one else can put it there."

Q; What is homophobia?

A: "Homophobia happens when, for no other reason, someone dislikes someone else just because they're gay. Homophobia is thankfully slowly decreasing, but it still exists. Some people are so homophobic that they express their hatred by bullying and even physically harming gays and lesbians."

Follow up

Many questions and concerns can and should come up as your child weaves their way through life. Let them know, regularly, that they can come to you anytime.

If it's important to them, it's important to you. Look them in the eyes when you say this. Keep learning so you can keep giving them accurate answers.

Keep the conversation going as the weeks and months unfold after your child asks a question. Discussing LGBTQ+ equality should not be a formal, once-and-done conversation. Encourage your child to keep asking questions.

In addition, the values you teach your child will be much more impactful if your discussions are sparked by family activities.

"Families have shared experiences, beliefs, and values that influence and enhance learning conversations."[6]

Integrate as many ongoing, casual conversations as you can into your shared family experiences.

HOW TO RAISE INCLUSIVE CHILDREN

Chapter 10.
Girls

The progress that's been made to ensure women can excel in their chosen field has been encouraging, but incredibly slow and arduous.

Regardless, equipping a generation of young girls with the confidence needed to grow successfully, without intimidation, remains a crucial priority.

> *In the article, "The Role of Parents in Inculcating Values," we learn "It takes time to acquire a habit, and parents need to be patient with their children. Keep repeating these habits every day so the child inculcates them more promptly. Sometimes, parents are not aware of what habits they should teach their children."* [20]

Yes, it takes time. But it's well worth the ongoing effort so parents can contribute to a future where girls are celebrated for their accomplishments.

To help, this chapter provides practical, day-to-day tips to boost girls gender-equality confidence.

Step 1. Start with the Basics

Define Gender Bias *Together*

The first step is to explain gender bias to your girl. You can start by telling her what *you* think it is.

So that she can understand it at her level, you could define it as:

"Sometimes in the classroom, teachers unintentionally show gender bias by allowing more boisterous behaviors from boys than girls, or expecting girls to turn in homework more consistently, or calling on boys more often to answer math questions."

Gauge her reaction here. Hopefully, she'll be nodding her head in agreement. Then, without putting her on the spot, ask her what she thinks *gender bias* is.

Really listen to her answer. Consider her words carefully before you react.

At this point in the conversation, it's extremely important for her to feel confident so that she believes in her ability to participate in the discussion.

Engage her participation but if her understanding of gender-equality is completely different from what you want her to know, reconsider your approach before you move on to the next section.

Help her understand that gender stereotypes are often completely false

When we hear something over and over again like "boys are better at math than girls" or "girls can't play sports," we tend to consider it as truth.

But just because something is said repeatedly, doesn't make it true. Your girl needs to know this.

To help your girl fully grasp the falsity of gender stereotypes, do an online search for girl powered TV shows and movies. Find something you can watch and discuss together that *defies* gender stereotypes.

If she's eager, let her come up with her own suggestions and watch them together. Encourage her to explain how her selection defies gender stereotypes.

Help her *discover* how entrenched gender bias is in our culture

Sometimes people aren't even aware they're being biased. Assuming women's inferiority has become so routine, it's *baked* into our culture.

> *Science Daily confirms the existence of hidden gender bias: "...stereotyped views are an instance of implicit bias, revealing automatic associations that people cannot, or at least do not, report holding when asked directly."* [21]

Media, and other cultural influences, perpetuate the bias that most people aren't even aware of. Here are some examples of common phrases that we often don't recognize as sexist:

- drama queen
- man up
- grow a pair
- throw like a girl
- don't you worry your pretty little head
- honey, dear, missy
- boys will be boys
- you guys

The list is endless. Girls need to know that this kind of unconscious gender bias blindly dictates everyday decisions, what the hidden meaning is, and how it affects them.

But just like the rest of the suggestions in this book, your message about unconscious bias will be more effective if your girl feels like she's discovered it on her own.

Here are some ideas for helping her *discover* unconscious bias:

- Explain why terms like *drama queen* are so insulting. But leave it at that. Encourage her to come up with more examples.

- Suggest that she start listening for gender-biased words and phrases in everyday conversations. You can get her started by watching a TV show together and calling attention to examples.

- Make it a game. Challenge her to come up with a list of everyday sexist phrases and gender-neutral alternatives. Tell her you'll do the same, and see whose list is longer. No online searching!

Let her come up with examples that support the definition that you have crafted together.

Just talking about ingrained gender inequality with you will hopefully guide her toward seeking out her own examples and clarifying it in her own mind.

Give her options for specific words she can use to respond to gender bias in her own life

Once you feel like your girl understands what gender bias is, why it's so demeaning, and how it's ingrained in our culture, it's time to help her respond to it.

For example, if she tells you there's a boy in her class who says she's not good at math because she's a girl, you could give her specific words to use.

If you give her enough options, she'll hopefully select the words that feel right for her. Here are some ideas for potential responses:

"Some girls are better than boys at some things, and some boys are better than girls at other things."

Or use humor:

"You just WISH you were as good at 'xyz' as I am."

Or simply:

"What made you say that? Can you explain it to me?"

Just pointing out the behavior without being accusatory can sometimes make a difference. Ask her what words she would use.

Give her as many options for responding as you can so she can pick the one she's most comfortable with. Work on the wording together.

Open, honest communication is key here.

Model confident behavior

> Try to remember that the purpose of the suggestions in this chapter is to help your girl understand that she is no less

important than a boy, that gender bias is completely unfounded, and that you are always available to help her respond to gender bias situations in her own life.

The best way to make these concepts sink in is by modeling confident behavior yourself. If she sees you reacting to outdated sexist notions by standing up for yourself, she'll mimic your behavior.

Conversely, if she sees you succumbing to outdated sexist norms, she'll assume that's what she should do too.

Media is another good way to drive home your message. Television shows are full of examples of gender bias. If you see something sexist on TV while you're watching a show together (or if it's just on in the background), make a comment about why it's offensive and bothersome to you.

Ask her if she heard it and if she thought it was acceptable. If she responds with an explanation that matches what you've already talked about and how she would respond, great.

If she doesn't respond, take the opportunity to explain why you think it's inaccurate, why it bothers you, and how you would respond.

Also, try not to be defensive if she starts calling you out on your own behavior. Her awareness means that your conversation sunk in. That's a good thing.

Thank her for pointing it out to you and tell her that you're going to work on fixing it. Ask her if she could remind you if she sees you doing it again.

Feeling like she's teaching *you* will help her absorb the concept, increase her awareness of gender bias, and clarify appropriate ways to respond.

If it feels like you're not getting anywhere, try again in a week or so. She needs to know that responding to gender bias is an important topic to you, that you want to share your feelings with her, and that it's significant enough for you to bring up again.

Note: Keep in mind that the suggestions in this chapter (and book) are meant to be communicated over a period of time, not in a single formal conversation.

Step 2. Provide Options for Helping Her Feel Included in Girl Power

At a time in your girl's life when feeling included and recognized is so important for her self-confidence, the girl-power movement offers a perfect opportunity to help her experience a sense of belonging and accomplishment.

She'll get to experience what it feels like to be included in a growing, unified goal, she'll get to discover and showcase her passion(s), and her self-esteem can grow exponentially.

Equally important, it's just as beneficial for introverts (independent thinkers) to feel a sense of belonging and forward movement as it is for extroverts (joiners). This section provides tips for both the independent thinker and the joiner.

Remember your girl needs to start the process of feeling included in the girl-power movement with someone she loves and trusts. You.

Talk about girl power *together*

This section's purpose is to get the process started of helping her feel included. Hopefully, she'll do the rest of the work on her own, but for now, she needs your help to get started.

First, offer your opinion about girl power and how you think it affects girls and women. Even though it's important to make this a conversation about her, it's also important to help her feel like you're sharing important personal information with her.

Doing your own sharing has the added benefit of guiding the conversation in the right direction.

Here are some questions you could ask if you're having a hard time getting things started:

- Do you think current efforts will affect women's rights for your generation?

- Do you think it's important to feel included in the current movement? (Note: tread lightly here—hopefully she'll answer *yes*.)

- Do you think girl power affects the women's rights movement?

Remember that the intent here is to elicit her opinions without putting her on the spot. At the same time, it's important for her to know that her thoughts and feelings matter. It's a delicate balancing act.

Also, her answers to your questions have two purposes: 1) they'll help you frame your strategy for implementing the rest of the tips in this chapter; and 2) they'll guide her thoughts toward feeling included in girl power.

Watch girl-power media *together*

Continue building shared opinions about girl power.

Watching a video together about a courageous woman is a great way to do this. It will let her organize her thoughts in private, without feeling like she has to form an opinion on demand.

Here are some options (available online) for things to watch together. We have vetted each item with age-appropriateness in mind, but of course the final decision is up to you.

Ask her to choose one (or more) after you have perused the list.

Documentaries

- **He Named Me Malala.** Features the young Pakistani female activist and Nobel Peace Prize laureate Malala Yousafzai, who spoke out for the rights of girls, especially the right to education.

- **Brave Girl Rising.** Tells the story of a courageous girl, inspired by the magical dreams of her mother and the sisterhood of her friends, succeed in getting the education she deserves.

Speeches

- **Priyanka Chopra.** Full Power of Women. This UNICEF ambassador and Bollywood actress gives an empowering speech about the importance of educating girls and giving a voice to the voiceless.

- **We Should All be Feminists by Chimamanda Ngozi Adichie.** In this TED talk, Chimamanda uses her experience growing up in Nigeria to highlight the misconceptions that have made the idea of equality between genders into something that it is not.

- **Meghan Markle UN Speech.** Meghan Markle recounts her experience as a young girl objecting to a P&G commercial about women washing dishes. In her speech, she uses her memory to reinforce the importance of standing up for what you believe in. **Note:** Meghan's age at the time of her epiphany (11 years old) will hopefully be an added incentive for your girl to feel connected to the notion of personal integrity.

Fictional movies with strong female lead(s):

- **Moana 2 (Disney).** The film continues the story of Moana, the strong-willed, heroic daughter of a chief of a Polynesian village, as she journeys to the far seas of Oceania after receiving an unexpected call from her way-finding ancestors.

- **Mulan (Disney).** Fearful that her ailing father will be drafted into the Chinese military, Mulan takes his spot—though, as a girl living under a patriarchal regime, she is technically unqualified to serve. She cleverly impersonates a man and goes off to train with fellow recruits. **Parent tip:** Mulan is a "Disneyfied," but dignified and accurate story of a brave, persistent Chinese girl warrior.

A Mighty Girl and Common Sense Media have more information about suitable movies.

HOW TO RAISE INCLUSIVE CHILDREN

Encourage her to join a girl's organization

At this point in your conversation, the subject of girl's organizations is appropriate to mention. If your girl is a joiner, there are some high-quality girl-power groups she can join.

If her preference is to do things on her own, there are also many proven, outstanding options available to help her feel like she belongs.

The list of girl groups below is for the joiner. The ensuing list of activities is for independent thinkers.

For girls who are at their best in a group setting, we recommend the following groups (all organizations listed here have either already established or are aspiring to establish chapters nationwide).

Note: This list is not exhaustive, but it will give you a good sense of the types of organizations that are available.

- **Global Girl Scouts.** A central focus of the Girl Scouts organization is raising strong and confident girls who are skilled leaders; this is emphasized through team-building activities and community service.

- **Girls on the Run International.** Girls on the Run fosters positive emotional, social, mental, spiritual, and physical development in girls ages eight to thirteen years old through running programs and workouts. The goal is to prevent girls from engaging in at-risk activities as they mature.

- **Global Girls.** Global Girls inspires girls worldwide to be strong, smart, and confident through education programs. Key programs include math and science education, drug abuse prevention, media literacy, economic literacy, adolescent health, violence prevention, and sports participation.

- **Girlstart.** Girlstart provides Science, Technology, Engineering and Math (STEM) education programs for girls in kindergarten through twelfth grade. This focus on STEM helps to develop interest in STEM electives, majors, and careers.

- **Girl Talk.** Girl Talk is a peer mentoring program that pairs high school girls with younger girls. The goal is to help younger girls navigate their tween and early teenage years. Not only do the younger girls benefit from the guidance of their older peers, but the high school girls also learn from sharing their experiences as positive role models.

- **Girls Leadership.** Girls Leadership considers girls' real-life, everyday relationships with friends and family as a prime opportunity to teach the leadership skills that will serve them over a lifetime: self-advocacy, negotiation, compromise, personal responsibility, and conflict as an opportunity for change. The Girls Leadership organization works not only with girls, but also with primary influencers (parents, teachers, and caregivers) to help girls develop leadership confidence, despite peer opinions. This is a great option for parents who want to transform their girl's "bossiness" into leadership skills.

- **Girl Up.** Girl Up is a campaign of the United Nations Foundation. The mission is to give girls the opportunity to become global leaders and to raise awareness and funds for United Nations programs that help adolescent girls in need around the world.

HOW TO RAISE INCLUSIVE CHILDREN

Suggest helping others as a way to help her feel empowered

This section includes ideas for your girl to feel included in the girl-power movement without forcing her to do something that she's not comfortable with, like joining a group.

Volunteering might be a smart way to facilitate her own confidence-building while simultaneously helping others. Any of the ideas below will help her feel empowered:

- Walk around the neighborhood with a garbage bag and pick up trash on the side of the road.

- In the fall, offer to rake leaves. In the winter, help shovel snow.

- Plant flowers for a neighbor or in a communal neighborhood area.

- Collect and deliver supplies to neighbors who have just had a baby, undergone surgery, or experienced a house fire.

- Coordinate a neighborhood garage sale and donate the proceeds to a local charity.

- Bring her with you to cook or serve meals at a homeless shelter.

- Make care packages for the homeless. Include travel-sized toiletries, granola bars, and bottled water.

- Collect coats and give them to a homeless shelter in winter.

- Gather canned foods to deposit at a local food bank.

- Have her sort through old toys she doesn't play with anymore and donate them to a local charity group.

- Participate in local events, such as 5Ks, fun runs, or other events that donate to local charities helping those in need.

- Volunteer at a local animal shelter.

- Donate newspapers, dog beds, or other pet supplies to a local animal shelter.

- Place bird feeders in the yard for local wild birds.

- Offer to walk a neighbor's dog.

- Pet sit for a neighbor when they go out of town.

- Bring smiles to local Senior Citizens by visiting or volunteering at an assisted living or nursing home facility.

- Bring easy-to-eat treats or hand-drawn cards to a nursing home or children's hospital.

- Decorate a senior center for a holiday.

- Read stories to younger children at libraries, daycare facilities, or churches.

- Offer to be a mother's helper to a new mom.

- Hold a lemonade stand or bake sale and donate the profits to a local organization.

- Bring meals to your local firehouse.

- Write thank you cards to local police officers and deliver them to the station to thank them for protecting the community.

- Volunteer at a Special Olympics event.

- Make gifts for children in the hospital, or distribute Halloween candy, Valentines, or Christmas gifts.

Be the spark!

'DEI for Parents' strives to make parents' lives more meaningful, *not* busier.

However, the only way to guide your girl toward feeling included in girl power *might very well be* daily inspiration and closeness with you. If so, here are some ideas:

- **Set daily reminders.** Motivational quotes are a great way to jumpstart a positive opinion of girl-power. The right quotes can remind your girl that girls are smart, capable, and deserve a chance to thrive. Take time to help her create daily reminders; there are plenty of smartphone apps that make it easy. She can use these reminders to begin her day on a positive girl-power note.

- **Be her biggest cheerleader.** Your girl needs to feel loved and supported at all times. Support her ideas and accomplishments by taking time to talk with her. Guide her toward confidence by being there to give her a little push when she needs it. Then stand back (a little) and watch her grow. Accomplishing a goal through her own hard work will show her that she is capable of creating her own confidence. So important!

- **Take a class together.** Do you know how to change a tire or fix the garbage disposal? If you do, pass this information on to your girl. If you don't, take a class and learn together. Teaching her to do fix-it chores around the house or how to change car tires are wonderful ways to boost her confidence.

- **Teach bravery.** Trying new things is a great way to learn bravery. Most of us develop confidence by experiencing mastery of a new skill that we were initially afraid to do or were simply unfamiliar with. When your girl is struggling with a new skill, remind her of the other times she's learned something new. Your guidance and encouragement will help her persevere.

- **Expose her to positive female role models.** There are countless women who are doing work that they are passionate about and making an impact in the world (yours truly included). Expose your girl to those you know in your daily life and those that you can find through film, television, and online sources. Point these amazing role models out to her whenever you can.

- **Try not to be too critical.** This is probably the trickiest suggestion, especially during the tween years. Your girl is pre-programmed to break away; it's a natural part of growing up. Try not to take it too personally. Guide her (as much as you can) to come up with her own solutions.

Step 3. Create a Gender-Equal Home Environment

Thanks to ongoing misogyny, it's more important than ever to create a gender-equal foundation at home so your girl can mimic equitable values, instead of antiquated notions, as she weaves her way through life.

Women have made *some* progress in this area, but not nearly enough. The article titled "*Girls spend 160 million more hours than boys doing household chores every day*" reveals more of this sad truth:

> The article titled "Girls spend 160 million more hours than boys doing household chores every day" reveals more of this sad truth: "The data show that the disproportionate burden of domestic work begins early, with girls between 5- and 9-years-old spending 30 percent more time, or 40 million more hours a day, on household chores than boys their age."[22]

Clearly, more improvement is sorely needed. The following suggestions are structured to help you cultivate a gender-equal household.

Chores

With chores, two principles are crucial for building an equitable household: 1) Children should help equally with household tasks regardless of gender; and 2) Both genders can and should help with both inside and outside chores.

First, try to keep in mind that chores are practice for adult living. If boys are allowed to continue playing video games while girls toil away in the kitchen, that's the model for fairness that your girl will take into adult life.

Second, try to refrain from assigning outside chores to boys (mowing the lawn) and inside chores to girls (emptying the dishwasher).

Girls need opportunities that not only stretch beyond traditional roles but also help build a foundation of self-sufficiency. If your girl learns how to mow the lawn now, she'll be better prepared for a gender-equal life as an adult.

It might take a few tries to perfect a task, and you might have to do some up-front heavy lifting/training, but that will eventually subside.

Of course, you know your children best and it's completely your decision to assign the appropriate amount and type of household chores based on developmental and physical ability.

That said, here are some ideas that defy the typical boy/girl chore assignments:

Boys:

- empty the dishwasher
- do the dishes
- make the dinner salad
- organize the grocery list
- feed the family pet(s)
- set the table
- vacuum
- sweep

HOW TO RAISE INCLUSIVE CHILDREN

- learn to use the washing machine and start a load of laundry
- fold laundry
- pick up clutter
- dust
- help care for baby and/or ailing grandparent

Girls:

- yard work—raking, weeding, mowing the lawn, etc.
- stack the firewood
- walk the dog
- unload grocery bags from car
- replace light bulbs
- empty indoor wastebaskets and recycle bins
- wheel outside trash and recycle cans to street
- wash windows
- collect dirty laundry from family members
- collect pet waste (if you have a yard and a dog)
- wash family car(s)
- clean garage
- auto repair

If your kid(s) complain about their tasks, listen to their protests, and ask how they would make it more equitable. Talk about it together. They need to feel like they're part of the equality discussion.

Ask if they think they can continue with their assigned chores for another week. Hopefully, they'll agree, their complaints will wane and then disappear altogether.

If not, you might consider rotating tasks, so everyone gets to try their hand at everything.

Repeat these words as often as you can:

"There's no such thing as boys' work or girls' work—it's all just work."

Allowance

Equal pay? Yes! Absolutely!

Not only does equal pay for equal work make practical sense, contribute to girls' self-esteem, and make it clear to both boys and girls that they are equally capable, there's another important benefit to consider.

> *Parent Map explains more: "Another advantage of chore equality and pay is that it teaches our daughters how to talk about money. Teaching them to negotiate a fair and equitable allowance can have lasting outcomes that would follow them into the working world, showing them that they deserve just as much money and respect as their male co-workers. This lesson is an important one."*[23]

Just like with chore assignments though, there might be some pushback to your allowance rules. If they start whining about who does more, listen to their concerns, ask how they would make it more equitable (without saddling you with more work or expense), and compromise.

It's important for them to know (especially your girl) that their opinion matters.

If there are special circumstances in any given week, e.g., special chores for bonus pay, sick child, conflicting family obligations, etc., try to balance out opportunities and payments in the following weeks.

Sibling arguments

Sibling squabbles are unavoidable. They come with the territory of being a parent to more than one child. And the long-overdue movement towards gender equality has introduced yet another reason for siblings to argue.

But it doesn't have to get nasty.

Yes, girls are starting to understand (hopefully!) that they are not the weaker gender. But that doesn't mean they need to be unkind about standing up for themselves.

Here are some ideas for guiding your girl toward standing up for herself and softening her message at the same time.

If you notice your girl using hostile language and/or gestures towards her brother (or whomever), take her aside and explain that being a gender-equal male is a fairly new concept and lots of boys need gentle guidance and time to adjust.

Tell her that patience is a learned skill and you're confident she is the right person to help him learn. Guide her toward helping him by being the teacher and using calm language.

The point of guiding your girl toward a teaching role is to give her back some of the autonomy that she feels like she lost.

Give her examples of calm language and understanding. Suggest that she use phrases like:

- *"That doesn't seem fair to me. Can we compromise so it's fair to both of us?"*

- *"What if I did that to you? Wouldn't you feel like I was being unfair?"*

- *"I already know how to xyz. You don't need to explain it to me. But thank you anyway."*

(Or use whatever language is appropriate.)

Let them talk through it on their own. Don't engage unless you feel like their conversation is headed in the wrong direction.

The goal here is to let them practice discussing the problem and reaching a compromise on their own. A valuable life skill!

If your girl still isn't making progress about whatever point she's trying to get across, tell her she can come to you, and you'll work it out together. She needs to know that she has a reliable, knowledgeable ally.

Model gender-equal household behavior

In an ideal world, both parents (if there are two) should be doing an equal amount of housework and both parents should be contributing the same amount of work hours outside the home.

But we don't live in an ideal world, and families come in all shapes and sizes, so the 50/50 scenario is a great goal, but not always realistic.

HOW TO RAISE INCLUSIVE CHILDREN

Whatever division of labor you and your partner can contribute towards the ideal 50/50 scenario is best.

Language

Try to keep in mind that although it might not seem obvious at the time, the words your girl hears and the actions she sees from you are etching a permanent opinion in her psyche.

For everyday conversations, try to use words that avoid gender bias. For example, the words policeman and stewardess are gender-specific job titles; the corresponding gender-neutral terms are police officer and flight attendant.

(You can always search the internet for gender biased language examples if you need more examples.)

Media

Another thing to be aware of is your attitude toward gender inequality in the media.

While you're watching the media resource together, make a remark about how fair or unfair a certain scene is. Then talk about how it used to be accepted that men were superior to women, but that mindset is thankfully changing.

Try to remain upbeat while you're saying this; there's no need to share your frustration about specific challenges.

Tell her how lucky she is to be young and alive during such an important movement toward equality and justice. The big picture is that opportunities for girls are finally headed in the right direction.

Make sure this concept sinks in. She needs to feel like this is a special time for her.

Toys/gadgets

Traditionally, the world of toys has been sexist. Most toy company marketing campaigns have been wrongly based on the theory that girls only play with creative or social toys and boys only play with spatial or digital toys.

The good news is that things are *slowly* changing. Many toy manufacturers are no longer explicitly marketing their products solely based on gender.

Retailers are starting to replace pink and blue toy aisles with gender-neutral toy aisles. Parents need to get on board too.

If you provide toys that are traditionally geared toward boys alongside toys that are traditionally geared toward girls, your girl will naturally gravitate toward the toy that appeals the strongest to her innate passions and capabilities.

Who knows? Maybe she's a born nurturer and will naturally gravitate toward dolls, but she should at least be given options.

Here are some toys that are traditionally associated with boys that should also be available to girls:

- construction vehicles
- Legos
- toy cars
- model airplanes/rockets
- magnetic building sets
- puzzles

- science kits
- sports equipment
- action figures
- train sets
- robots
- binoculars
- microscopes
- remote-control racing/flying devices

Electronic gadgets, e.g., smart phones, tablets, laptops, etc., follow the same guidelines as gender-based toys.

Use an online shopping resource to let your girl choose the gadget "flavor" that appeals to her. If she wants the laptop decorated with the solar system instead of ballerinas, let her have it.

Step 4. Explain Consent at Her Level So She Feels Like She Owns It

Thanks to the #metoo movement and the long-overdue disclosure of rampant, harmful misogyny, consent has *finally* become a recognized value that needs to be taught to our children.

One way to teach consent is to explain it to girls at their level by equating it with respect, self-respect, and boundaries.

To do that, the tips in this section are intentionally ordered sequentially to take you step-by-step through the process of helping your girl fully comprehend *respect,* then *self-respect,* and then *boundaries.*

Further, each tip's content is intentionally designed to help your girl feel ownership of the subject as you're teaching.

> *According to the article "Let Children Lead," "The more you hand over to the children, the more they feel in control of their learning. By giving them ownership, I find children develop a love for learning. It is empowering for children to see their brilliant ideas come to fruition."*[24]

Hopefully as the years unfold, she'll feel more and more of an ownership of *consent*. And the more ownership she feels, the easier it will be for her to apply the values you teach to scenarios in her own life as she grows.

Review basic respect *together*

Start by giving her a compliment and saying something like:

"I know you already know what respect is. For starters, it's things like saying 'please' and 'thank you.' And I know you already know that respect goes beyond just saying 'please' and 'thank you.'"

To me, respect is a way of treating or thinking about something or someone. If you respect your teacher, you admire her and treat her well. If you respect your friend, you regard her highly and treat her with consideration."

Hopefully, she'll chime in here and add her own examples of respect. If she doesn't contribute and needs more time to join the conversation, you could continue offering your own examples about what respect is.

Try to tailor your examples to match activities in her life. For example, you could say something like,

"Respect is not interrupting the teacher or not borrowing someone's sweater without asking."

HOW TO RAISE INCLUSIVE CHILDREN

Keep it simple. Talking about it with her on a level that she understands will greatly increase the odds that the concept sinks in. If you start throwing around terms like *sexual assault* and *social injustice*, she's likely to tune out.

The goal at this point is simply to establish a foundation by helping her feel comfortable with the topic of consent and contribute her own ideas as much as possible.

Keep the conversation going by defining respect together. Try to get her to expand on your examples. Then expand on her examples so it starts (or continues) to feel like a two-way conversation.

Here are more ideas for defining respect together:

- Think of someone who is respectful and talk about why they would be a good friend.

- Think of things people say who are respectful. Here are a few: "please," "thank you," "I appreciate that," "May I hold the door for you?," "Excuse me," and "I'm sorry I offended you."

- Respect for belongings is a big issue at this age. You could try to integrate it into the conversation if you're having a hard time getting things started. If you're the target of her "respect for belongings" frustration (for example, you borrowed something from her without asking), listen attentively to her feelings, make eye contact, and tell her you'll pay more attention to the problem and work on improving.

- Watch a TV show together and point out examples of respect/disrespect and why. Do the same thing when you're out doing errands together (store clerks? parking etiquette? check-out line?).

- Think of ways to show respect that connect with her interests. For example, if she's interested in climate change, think of examples (together!) that respect the environment. Recycling? Reducing carbon emissions? Look up Rachel Carson and/or Laurie David on Wikipedia and talk about how they respect the environment. Or guide the conversation toward a young person by talking about Greta Thunberg or someone from her social circle.

Try to make sure she has a good foundation for understanding respect before continuing.

Connect respect and self-respect

One way to pivot the conversation from respect to self-respect is to connect both terms by discussing simple definitions of self-respect together.

Here are some ideas for simple definitions:

- When you set boundaries that you don't let others cross.

- When you accept yourself for who you are, no matter what others say.

- When you feel good about yourself and know you deserve to be treated fairly.

Let her tell you which definition she likes the best. Remember, you want her to feel like she has an equal stake in the conversation.

HOW TO RAISE INCLUSIVE CHILDREN

Play a game where you both think of everything you love about yourself. You can start by listing the wonderful things about yourself. This will allow her to clearly see your own self-love and will give her permission to do the same.

When it's her turn and she shares things that she likes about herself, discuss it with her extensively.

Maybe she'll tell you that she always keeps her word to others. She considers herself very reliable because she always does what she says she's going to do.

Or maybe she considers herself to be trustworthy because when someone tells her something confidential, she keeps it a secret.

Whatever she tells you, the goal here is to make a big deal about the traits she considers admirable about herself.

Then connect the traits she admires about herself with self-respect.

Give her an example of when you chose to respect your own boundaries. Maybe someone tried to cut you off in the Starbucks line or the grocery store line. Tell her that your inner dialogue said *"Wait. That's not fair to me."*

Without putting her on the spot, ask her if she can think of an example of someone who tried to cross her boundaries, and she stuck up for herself.

When she offers her own example, pay extra attention to it. Ask her what made her decide it wasn't fair to her, what she said/did, and what was the outcome?

Dwell on her decision to respect herself so your girl gets a healthy dose of experiencing what self-respect feels like. This is a great opportunity for the concept of self-respect to fully sink in.

Another suggestion is for you to find a role model who exudes self-respect and point out that person (Beyoncé? Lady Gaga? Someone from her world? Someone you both know?).

Even if the role model you point out seems obnoxiously self-involved, talk about how you can tell that person would never let anyone take advantage of her.

The goal of this last suggestion is to give your girl a visual example of self-respect—someone she could hypothetically ask herself "Would Lady Gaga let someone do that to her? Probably not."

Continue to think of ways, together, that you can practice self-respect as you go about your busy lives.

Return to the topic and compare notes. She might have more questions as she goes out into the world and practices what you discussed.

Take time to answer her questions thoroughly. Make it an ongoing conversation.

Define boundaries together

One of the more important building blocks of successful parenting is establishing and maintaining consistent boundaries. But because boundaries is such an abstract concept, when explaining it to your girl, it's best to use an easily identifiable visual metaphor.

For example, you could equate *parental* boundaries as a long bowling alley lane with a rubber bumper on each side where your girl can zigzag from one bumper (boundary) to the other and feel safe.

As she progressively tests the limits of her world, she'll hopefully feel safe every time she bounces off one boundary and encounters another. As she grows, her boundaries will get farther and farther apart.

HOW TO RAISE INCLUSIVE CHILDREN

The same bowling alley metaphor can be used to help your girl understand the concept of boundaries as she applies them to her own independence.

Tell her that as she gets older, she will be increasingly in charge of how far to expand (or not) her own personal boundaries of consent.

She needs to know that she, and she alone, is in charge of controlling the boundaries for how others treat her.

Depending on your girl's maturity level, here are some more words from the article "Teaching Kids How to Set & Protect Their Boundaries Against Toxic Behavior" from Hey Sigmund that you could use to explain boundaries:

- *"We all have a thing around us called a boundary, which is a line between ourselves and other people. You can't see it but it's there. It's kind of like an invisible forcefield and it's there to protect each of us from the people who feel bad to be around—the ones who say mean things or do mean things that you just don't deserve."*[25]

- *"You are completely in charge of the invisible forcefield around you. You can decide when it goes up and when it comes down. You can decide what's allowed in and what must stay out. You're the boss of yourself and you'll always be the boss."*[25]

- *"Sometimes there might be people who do or say mean things so often that you never feel good when you're around them. That's when it's okay to put your forcefield up. In fact, it's one of the bravest things you can do."*[25]

- *"It's important to respect other people, but it's even more important to respect yourself first—and putting up your forcefield is one of the ways you can do this."*[25]

- *"We can't control other people, but we can control whether we let the mean things they say or do come close enough to hurt us. Being a kid is hard work—and you're awesome at it."*[25]

- *"Everyone is responsible for how they treat other people, including grownups, but the person you have to treat the very best is yourself. Sometimes that means not listening to what other people might say about you."*[25]

- *"Sometimes you have to be your own hero and protect yourself from being hurt by people who don't know the rules about being kind and respectful."*[25]

Any combination of the suggested words above will help communicate to your girl how important boundaries are.

Model respectful behavior

As with *all* values we try to instill in our children, the best way to get the message across is by modeling the behavior ourselves.

While your girl is gradually mulling over respect, self-respect, and boundaries in her own head, she needs someone she can emulate.

Here are some suggestions for what you can do and say that will give your girl someone she loves and trusts (you!) to mimic:

- **Keep your cool.** Instead of yelling, *"Don't you say that to me, it's disrespectful!"*, calmly respond to her misbehavior with words like "*You know, we don't talk to each other like that in our family. We treat each other with respect.*"

- **Practice kind and firm discipline.** Discipline means to teach or to train, not to punish. It's not about shaming her. Discipline is a lot more effective and longer lasting when you don't use punitive strategies. Teaching respect and using disrespectful discipline are mutually exclusive.

- **Reiterate that everyone is different.** When children's differences are accepted, they feel heard and respected. If she has a different way of doing things, respect that difference by saying things like "*I've never seen anyone do it that way before, but I like it!*" Use the words "*everybody's different*" every opportunity you get.

- **Don't be disrespectful of others.** Children are master observers. If you're sarcastic, dismissive, and talk behind others' backs, she'll try out that kind of behavior soon enough. If she thinks it's OK to be disrespectful of others and to herself, she'll mimic your behavior.

- **Model positive personal ethics.** Whether it's obvious or not, she's watching you. She's watching and listening to things like whether you pay your bills on time, if you help others, if you're generous with tips when the waiter/waitress does a good job, and if you participate in charitable giving.

- **Say you're sorry if you screw up.** A mature, respectful grownup accepts responsibility and apologizes when he or she makes mistakes. Let her see and hear you apologizing if you are wrong.

- **Share your own story.** This will make her feel like you're accessible and that she has a starting point for a conversation about self-respect. For example, she might say something like *"Remember when you told me xyz, well something similar happened to me and I need your opinion."*

- **Show respect to your partner.** This will go a long way towards setting an example of how two people should treat each other. Remember she's watching you. Even things like whether it's OK to take/use another person's belongings without asking is something she'll learn from you.

- **Be a good listener.** Give her your undivided attention when she is speaking to you. Listening to others' opinions without retaliation is an enormous part of learning how to respect others.

- **Be trustworthy.** Keep her heart-felt feelings and experiences private; show her that you can be a trusted adult who cares about her feelings and her self-respect.

- **Go on a date together.** Dads? Uncles? Consider taking your girl on a date to show her how she should expect to be treated. She needs to feel empowered and know that a healthy relationship is free from hurt (emotionally and physically) and behaviors like that are unacceptable. Shower her with love, appreciation, and respect and ideally, she will expect the same from her future partners.

Granted, the modeling suggestions above are extremely hard to accomplish, especially when you're in the heat of the moment.

But if you can at least strive to accomplish *some* of the suggestions, your girl will be better off. It will help her define *respect* in her own head and will also help her recognize when disrespect is occurring in her own life.

Make consent an ongoing conversation

While she's young, sex doesn't necessarily have to be part of the conversation. The subject of consent can be anything related to how two people treat each other.

As she grows older, you can modify the subject. For example, when she's 7, your consent conversation might be about a friend who borrowed her sweater without asking.

As she gets older, the consent subject can slowly wind its way into lots of more mature topics of conversation. If the conversation is about sex, she needs to know that she doesn't have to do anything with her body (or anything else that belongs to her) that she doesn't want to.

Even if all she hears from your ongoing conversations is "blah blah blah consent blah blah blah self-respect blah blah blah," you've given her two words (*self-respect* and *consent*) she can use as a takeaway.

Hopefully, none of your conversations will sound like "blah blah blah." But if she comes back to you a few days later and says, "*what's consent again?*" you've done your job.

Keep hammering away at the notion of self-respect and consent. She needs words she can use as a reminder of your conversation.

Remember though, kids are clever. When you think you're sneakily slipping "consent" into the conversation, she might be fully aware of what you're doing. (Just a heads up.)

The good news is that the decisions that she makes as she grows through adolescence and early adulthood will be informed by her understanding of what you teach her in your ongoing conversations about self-respect.

If you can get her to remember your discussion of consent when she's unsure about boundaries, she'll be one step ahead.

Step 5. Guide Her Toward Discovering and Exploring Her Passion

Having a passion that your girl can pursue wholeheartedly and rely on to always be by her side throughout her life, will be a huge advantage for her.

There are many ways you can guide her toward discovering and exploring that passion without being obvious about it. Here are some ideas.

Offer multiple activities

Give her options galore!

She needs to experience a full sampling of everything that's available to her. If she's never given the opportunity to explore a myriad of possibilities, she'll never know what lights the spark inside her.

Most community centers offer classes for kids in multiple subjects. Get a copy of your community center pamphlet and, with your girl, look through the classes/activities that are offered.

There should be options for music, sports, dance, cooking, art, carpentry, writing, computers, etc. Which activities interest her? Ask her to choose one and then sign her up.

The more activities she experiences, the greater her chance of discovering her true passion. If she gravitates toward a particular activity, ask her (subtly) what she likes about it and if she wants to find out more.

If she's on the shy side, and prefers to experience activities with someone she loves and trusts, when it's safe, go to discovery museums, sports events, musicals, book signings, movies/documentaries, dance performances, etc.

Anything that will expose her to a wide spectrum of interests.

Or maybe you could clear your schedule on a Saturday to do an activity of your girl's choice and ask her why she wanted to go on that particular outing. If you notice that she has a new area of interest, ask her what it is that specifically fascinates her about this topic.

Learning what's at the root of your girl's passion can help you direct her to similar activities she might enjoy too.

Watch and listen. If you notice that her interest is sparked by a particular activity, subtly ask her leading questions like *"what was your favorite part?"* and/or *"why was xyz your favorite part?"*.

Hopefully, these kinds of questions will trigger her brain to start digging deeper into whatever activity interests her. Let her have private thoughts so she feels like she's discovering her passion on her own.

If there is a subject that you notice she is particularly interested in, you have a wonderful head start. Ask her if she wants to find out more about that subject.

Note: It's also possible that she doesn't have an interest yet that she's passionate about. Her brain might not be ready to narrow things down.

As she grows, there will be plenty of opportunities for her to discover something that lights her spark. Everyone's pace is different. Let some time pass before you offer more options.

Let her be bored

If you hear your girl say "I'm booooored!" that's a good thing.

Boredom is the perfect outlet for her to get creative and find imaginative ways to entertain herself. It's also the perfect time for you to watch and listen to whatever activity she naturally gravitates to.

Boredom is so important to self-exploration, in fact, that it's wise to purposely create scenarios for your girl where she has no pre-planned activities.

> *In the article "5 Ways Boredom Makes Your Kid More Awesome," we learn "When our kids have nothing to do, they exercise their imaginations and that just might be the most important skill they can develop."*[26]

Try to steer her away from watching television (or any screen) and take notice of what she does.

Does she head toward the kitchen and put together a snack or meal? Does she go outside and ride her bike? Build a makeshift treehouse? Explore with a neighborhood pal? Brush the dog?

Does she stay inside and read? Write? Crafts? Hang on you? Test limits?

Can she successfully entertain herself? If so, it will boost her problem-solving skills and self-esteem. If not, ask her what her favorite thing to do is. Guide her toward that activity (or reasonable replicas).

Whatever she does, try carving out downtime for more than one day and keep watching to see where her mind goes.

Her natural inclinations won't necessarily scream "this is my passion!" but they might lead to a larger picture of her personality tendencies.

For example, if she repeatedly gravitates toward caring for the family dog (brushing, throwing a ball, comforting, etc.), maybe she's a natural caretaker? A veterinarian/psychologist/teacher in training? Maybe.

Or does she gravitate toward building something? (It could even be rearranging rocks in the yard.) Future engineer or architect?

Try to make a mental note of what she does and see if any other "Ah-ha!" activities or trends come to mind. Watch and listen.

If you notice a pattern, great. But don't make it obvious that you've been watching her.

It's so important for her to feel like she's discovering herself on her own. Your job is to provide the right space and time for her to grow into herself.

Take her to work with you

If you work somewhere that allows you to take your girl for a visit, schedule some time to do just that. Sharing your own likes and dislikes will allow her to start thinking about what she's truly passionate about.

Tell her why you got into the line of work that you did and what you were good at as a kid. Kids love learning about their parents' past.

Are there parts of your job when the time goes by really quickly because you're doing something you love? Tell her about it. Share with her what parts of your job you like and dislike and why.

As long as you're setting a positive example, that whole "monkey see, monkey do" thing can be a benefit here. Some passions are born out of a desire to model the interests and behaviors of the people your girl loves and admires.

If you have female relatives or friends with professions that you think might interest your girl, ask them if they're willing to share. Your girl will hopefully love seeing what you and others do at work all day.

Again, let her have private thoughts so she feels like she's discovering her passion on her own. But be sure to answer any questions she asks.

Sharing professional day-to-day tasks will either increase your girl's desire to be more like you or will make her realize she doesn't want to go down the same path you did. Either way, that realization is important to her self-discovery.

Nurture her interests

You might not know until she is older, but once you start to see your girl's natural talents develop, it's important to nurture them. The innate gift(s) that she is born with should be celebrated and supported.

When you realize that your girl has a particular interest, you should encourage her (without being too obvious about it) to explore it further. Guide her toward participating in specific activities, watching relevant TV shows, or going on educational outings.

Does she love cars? Take her to a car show. Or maybe she just can't stop talking about chess. Seek out a club where she can practice her chess skills.

If she's always talking about basketball and shooting hoops every chance she gets, sign her up for any basketball-related activities you can find.

HOW TO RAISE INCLUSIVE CHILDREN

Whatever she's interested in at the moment, and it could change suddenly and repeatedly, lead her down a path that offers the opportunity to learn more. Even if that path is a dead-end, keep offering opportunities.

Here are more ideas for guiding her toward exploring her passion:

- Research YouTube e-learning tutorials.

- Look for books that she might be interested in.

- Do an online search for your girl's passion followed by the words "activities for girls" in "your location." For example, enter "writing activities for girls in San Francisco" and click through the search results.

- Ask her teachers, friends' parents, neighbors, and family members if they know of any resources that would be appropriate for your girl to explore her passion.

- Join a Facebook or Instagram group for parents and ask if anyone in the group knows of a good resource in your area (or online) for your girl to explore her passion.

- Sign your girl up for a summer camp (with her involvement of course) that focuses on her passion.

- Go together on trips to museums, galleries, sports events, and festivals that celebrate your girl's passion.

- If your girl wants to explore her passion by starting her own business, there are lots of girlpreneur examples and resources online. The Startup Squad is a good place to start.

- Look for magazines and online newsletters that you think your girl might like to receive regularly.

Be patient. She's learning. Try to step back and let her explore at her own pace.

Definitely don't let her know you have an end-goal in mind. Just keep quietly offering exposure to activities that complement her interests.

If she takes a roundabout route, that's OK. Let her know you support her every step of the way.

Take a step back

Once you locate the right resource(s), it's really important to let her do the rest of the legwork on her own. Let her choose the details that she thinks fit her best.

As long as her choice is safe and doesn't conflict with other family obligations, support her decision. She still needs to know that you're there to continue guiding her in the right direction.

The simple fact that you're willing to take time out of your own busy schedule to find appropriate resources shows that you're interested in her well-being.

Involve her in the research process so she knows you're looking for activities to support her passion. Guide her toward feeling a sense of ownership.

Step 6. Creating a Dedicated Project Space Just for Her

As girls and women are (slowly!) starting to take their rightful places in an historically male-dominated world, it's so important for your girl to feel like she has every right to pursue her interests.

Helping her feel like she has a space of her own to navigate her abilities at her own pace will not only reinforce the notion to her and to your entire family that her development is important but will also enable her to investigate her own special abilities with confidence.

Find a space *together* that she can call her own

Even if your girl has her own room, she needs a project space to call her own that is part of the family area of your home. Situating her space in a common area has the benefit of sending a message to the entire family that her work is an integral part of the household.

Find a spot together that she can call her own. It doesn't have to be big or elaborate. It could even be an unused nook, wall space, a closet, a foyer, a play space, or a corner.

Just an area that is solely hers where she knows that her ideas and activities are safe. Make sure that the entire family understands the boundaries of her space.

It should be clear that you have the final say about what space will work best. That said, try to involve your girl in your thought process as much as possible.

With her input, try to find a space where she's within earshot of an adult family member, so she can ask questions, feel like she is an important part of the family, and get help if there's an emergency.

Make her feel included now; you'll be happy you did when the time comes to clean up after a messy project.

Include the basics

The goal of this project-space is to create a sense of independence for your girl. The contents of the space that you create for her aren't as important as the fact that you are showing her that she matters enough for you to take the time and energy to do right by her.

That said, there are some considerations for what to include in her special spot.

At the very least, she needs a table, a chair, a light, an electrical outlet, and a trash can. These bare necessities should be enough to provide a foundation for most activities.

To provide a space beyond the bare necessities, her table could have drawers or open spaces for storage bins, there could be some kind of shelving or peg board for storing tools and project supplies.

There could be a power strip, a rolling utility tray, table-top containers, a spot for her laptop or tablet if she has her own, and a drop-cloth or plastic sheeting for messy projects.

There should also be empty space on either side of her area in case she needs room for future expansion as her interests evolve.

Pinterest is a great source for project space ideas. Here are some of the search terms you could use both on online and on the Pinterest search engine to find what you need:

- at home kids tinker space
- DIY workbench

- home project table for kids

Make sure she helps

You should not set up a designated space for your girl's activities without her help; she should be involved in every step of the process.

Her involvement will not only give her a sense of ownership and independence, but it will also hopefully take some of the onus off you.

If she resists helping, you could tell her that you can't set it up without her help because you don't know exactly what kind of layout would work best for her projects.

Tell her she'd be much better at designing the space than you would be (flattery still works at this age!).

If she continues to resist helping, show her a calendar and ask her to pick a day and time that would be good for her to set up her project space with you.

Once you agree on a day and get started, encourage her to help you with the "heavy lifting," e.g., moving furniture, sweeping or vacuuming newly vacant spots, going with you to the store for a power strip, replacing light bulbs, etc.

As with all projects with kids, it will go much faster if she is actually helping and not creating more work along the way.

If all goes well, you should be able to complete it together in an afternoon.

Let her customize her space

It's time for you to take a break and for your girl to customize her space to fit her needs and personality.

As long as she doesn't want to make any permanent structural changes to your home, let her personalize the space on her own. Create a list together of future supply *wants* and budget guidelines.

> *Greenpath Financial Wellness suggests: "Talk with your child about money and how to use it wisely. Talk about their goals for their money. What do they want? What do they need? There may be short-term goals they can be purchased right away. They may have long-term goals that will require them to save over time. It is helpful for children to have a reminder of why they are saving and why they should not spend all of their money now."*[27]

Teaching your girl about prioritizing her *wants* for her project area is a great way for her to learn about budgeting and becoming financially independent later in life.

Schedule a trip to the Dollar Store together. Or here are some ideas for items she could find around the house:

- paper towels
- Kleenex
- pencils
- pens
- empty cans or jars to hold supplies
- Sharpies
- wet wipes
- Popsicle sticks

- old carpet remnants
- glue sticks
- baby food containers
- coffee filters
- paper plates
- clothes pins
- scissors
- masking tape
- duct tape
- aluminum foil
- cardboard toilet paper and paper towel tubes
- hand towels
- old flat sheet for messy projects

Gather some of these items and tell her you trust her to organize her space on her own. Encourage her to make her space functional to fit her needs.

This is a perfect time for you to take a break.

Establish ground rules

Your girl will hopefully be displaying some mixture of gratitude and awe at this point—gratitude that she has a spot to call her own and awe that you're taking time out of your busy schedule to help set it up with her.

As with any new ownership, however, comes a new set of responsibilities. She should know that her new space comes with rules.

Tell her that you have informed the other family members that her space is hers only and they're not to touch it. If there is ever a controversy about someone invading her space, ask her to come to you so you can resolve it together.

However, let her know, gently, that it's not okay for her to be bossy/dictatorial about her space. Yes, it's hers and hers alone but she lives in a household not a personal cubicle.

Remind her that she's responsible for upkeep if she wants to continue calling it her personal project space. Here are some things that might need doing as her activities evolve:

- replace light bulb on table lamp
- replace paper towel roll or clean rag
- maintain clean work area
- empty trash can
- save allowance/money for any accessories/tools she wants to add

Tell her it's now her own personal project area. Enjoy!

If your girl's project space becomes a positive part of her development, think of other ways her space can be used and/or expanded as she gets older.

Step 7. Help Her Find the Right Role Model

Thanks to the internet and the increasing visibility of women excelling in professional careers, your girl can easily find and follow a pertinent example.

Discoverability is key here. Finding the right role model can make the difference between discovering her gender-equality confidence and not even trying.

Once she locates someone whom she admires and wants to emulate, your girl can investigate her role model's path to success and set similar goals for herself. (Maybe she doesn't have to look very far because you're her role model! If so, congrats to you!)

Ideally, because her role model was able to find success, she'll believe that she can be successful too.

This section focuses on explaining the importance of role models to your girl, focusing on the subject that interests her, and helping her find a role model who exemplifies the kind of success she looks up to.

Explain why role models are important

First, helping your girl understand the importance of role models is crucial to engaging her in the role model search process.

You can start by talking up the benefits of role models in general. The slogan, "If you can see it, you can be it," is often used to define the importance of role models.

It's a memorable (and lighthearted) phrase and might be a good way to get things going.

> *According to the article "What is a Role Model?," "Role models show young people how to live with integrity, optimism, hope,*

determination, and compassion. They play an essential part in a child's positive development."[28]

After you feel like the concept of role models and their importance has sunk in with your girl, tell her that this is the perfect time in history for her to find a role model.

Tell her how lucky she is to have been born when female role models are not only more plentiful, but the internet has made it extremely easy to find them.

Note: Role models are often confused with mentors. A good explanation of the difference is that a mentor knows you and tries to help you succeed; you have an actual two-way relationship with a mentor. Alternately, a role model is someone whom you look up to and try to emulate from afar; it's a one-way connection.

Ask her what subject most interests her

So that your girl can find a role model who has the same interests as hers, she'll need to decide on her favorite subject.

Maybe she already knows what lights her spark or maybe she doesn't. Either way, knowing which subject captures her interest will make it much easier to find the right role model.

Tell her a little about what subject captured your interest when you were younger and why. Then prompt her to explain to you what subject she's most interested in and why.

Your girl's decisions about her interests might change many times during her growing-up years. The important thing is for her to know that you are consistently interested in her development.

Having conversations with you about her favorite subject will hopefully help her clarify her own opinions and identify a role model who is succeeding in a subject that interests her.

Guide her toward online role model websites

If your girl doesn't have a role model readily available in her immediate circle, there are some safe online sites where she can find what she's looking for.

Even though initial contact is made on these sites via the potential role model's contact information, if you haven't already, now is a good time to have that conversation with your daughter about not giving out her personal information online.

As she gets older, her choice of her role model might change. But for now, guide her toward the person who exemplifies the characteristics and expertise she looks up to.

Here are some resource ideas:

- **Fab Fems (STEM-specific).** Fab Fems are women from a broad range of professions in science, technology, engineering, and mathematics (STEM). They have signed up to be part of the Fab Fems directory specifically to be role models for young girls.

- **25 Female Role Models in History Every Kid Should Know.** This website lists 25 outstanding female role models in history. The list includes information about why your kids should know about them and links to resources where you can learn more.

- **Rebel Girls app.** This is a free app that immerses girls into audio stories about the adventures and accomplishments of women from around the world and throughout history, including incredible women who are active today.

- **Common Sense Media** is a wonderful resource for finding movie and television show role models who are appropriate for your girl's age and interests. Once you're on their website, enter "role model" into the search field at the top of the home page, and scroll through the search results to find appropriate media.

Share this information with your girl without sounding too obvious. Remember, the goal is to guide.

Exposing her to as many successful women as possible can never go wrong. Give her several options and let her make her own decision.

Step 8. Encourage STEM Thinking at Home

Relating STEM principles to everyday household projects, conversations, and media choices is a great way to boost your girl's STEM knowledge and confidence.

And who knows? She might actually embrace STEM concepts even more when they involve doing something fun.

The options below should give you a good start for discovering informal STEM-learning opportunities in your own home.

Note: Even though the ideas in this step provide suggestions for encouraging and maintaining girls' interest in STEM subjects, many of the principles can be applied to non-STEM subjects as well.

Relate STEM concepts to whatever she's into

Here are some ideas for connecting her interests with STEM concepts.

- If she likes to cook, you could talk about recipe measurements and/or scientific food reactions.

- If she's into mixing weird ingredients together, make a DIY bubble mixture and discuss how the ingredients interact. (This one could possibly get messy. Just a heads up.)

- If she loves ballet, have her think about how pointe shoes are engineered to support the human skeleton.

- If she has a fish tank, talk about how plants provide oxygen and absorb the carbon dioxide and ammonia that fish generate.

- If she likes to help people with disabilities, you could talk about 3D printing and artificial limbs.

If you need more information about a topic, you can supplement your knowledge with a simple online search. All you need to do is search the word for her passion followed by "STEM" (e.g., "ballet STEM") and spend a few minutes reading and clicking around to find information that you think might capture her interest.

Encourage problem-solving and perseverance

The very act of recognizing a problem and seeking a better result is STEM in action.

In all STEM subjects, finding out that something doesn't work is just as important as discovering a new way to make it work.

For example, suppose your girl doesn't consider herself a good bike rider. The next time she complains that she can't go as fast as everyone else, encourage her to use the word *yet* at the end of her sentence.

Explain to her that everything takes practice; no one is instantly good at anything. Tell her if she keeps practicing riding her bike, even if it feels frustrating and pointless at first, she'll eventually be able to go faster, or whatever she feels is holding her back.

Praise effort over results. Tell her to keep at it.

> As explained by the Bright Horizons Education Team, praise is a big deal: "Offer praise and encouragement for your child's effort. We tend to praise our children for being smart, but also remember to offer encouragement for completing goals, for not giving up, and for being determined."[29]

Help her make the mental connection between her bike-riding practice and the importance of finding better solutions, persisting, tweaking assumptions, adjusting actions, and discovering new and improved results. STEM in action.

If you can successfully convince your girl that determination is part of learning, not only have you highlighted the STEM concept of viewing challenges as opportunity, but you've also taught her a crucial life lesson about the importance of persistence and not doubting yourself.

Pick the right media

As we all know, the media has an enormous influence on what we absorb on a daily basis. Here are some suggestions for making sure your girl is absorbing the right thing:

Television. Try to watch a show together. When you do, encourage STEM-related shows. Talk about the program you viewed afterwards. Common Sense Media has some great choices for educational TV shows for kids.

Movies. Again, Common Sense Media has outstanding suggestions for STEM-related movies you can watch together.

(**Note**: Common Sense's movie list is intended for classroom discussions, but the movies are available for home streaming too.)

Websites. There are lots of wonderful STEM websites available now for helping girls improve their STEM skills. All you have to do is search online for "STEM activity websites" to find a long list.

The trick is to figure out which websites are educationally advantageous and safe. Here are some tips on what to look for:

- Is the content current? A good way to tell is to look at dates. If one of the main activities is more than 6-9 months old, the website is probably outdated.

- Is the resource for girls only? While it's important for girls to feel empowered by girls-only resources, you shouldn't discount a high-quality STEM website just because it's not solely for girls.

- How long has the organization been in operation? While the surge of support for STEM girls is fairly recent and there are some perfectly fine newer resources, if you have a choice between a newish resource and an established quality-driven one, pick the established quality-driven one.

- Negative reviews? Do an online search for reviews. If the resource has a bad review, even if it sounds like it's from a chronic complainer, move on. There are plenty of other choices.

- Does the resource focus on career advancement? At some point in the future, your girl will need to start angling her

STEM interest(s) towards a viable career, but not yet. If the website looks like it's career-focused only, remove it from your list.

Step 9. Infuse Life Lessons into Science-Fair Stress (or *Any* Project Competition)

Girls seem to experience a disproportionate amount of stress at science fairs (or *any* project competition). Not only are they on the spot to outperform their peers, but they're also starting at a runner-up position because they're girls.

But science fairs aren't necessarily all about stress and winning. There are some hidden life-experience gems too, e.g., committing to a decision, managing time, making assumptions, etc.

Working through these life lessons together can be a wonderful way for you to teach (or reteach) skills that strengthen your girl's odds for future success.

Here are some ideas for teachable moments:

Make good decisions. It's important for your girl to select a project topic carefully, make a commitment, and stick with it. This project could potentially be the longest project she has experienced. Help her choose a topic that is both interesting to her and is also robust. Easy projects might seem appealing at first, but she'll regret her decision if six weeks into the project, her content is weak, and she realizes that she picked a "skinny" topic. Bonus points for selecting a topic that sparks future ideas.

Lay the groundwork before you start a project. It's so tempting to start a project without being fully prepared. We've all done it at some point and had to start all over. Science fair projects are no different.

HOW TO RAISE INCLUSIVE CHILDREN

Help your girl understand how important it is to research reliable information sources *before* she starts her project. One way to establish and organize research methods is to start a project journal where she can list information sources and what type(s) of data they provide.

Manage your time efficiently. Science fair projects are perfect learning experiences for the importance of effective time management. Using a calendar to plan project milestones is a wonderful visual tool for honing this life lesson. Help your girl use the calendar to block out time for research, supply purchases, trial and error, family commitments, report writing, display board creation, practicing her speech, etc. Make sure she adjusts the calendar as the project unfolds.

Set a budget and stick to it. Science fair projects are a perfect opportunity to help your girl get a head-start on learning how to budget money. Once she selects a project topic, she'll have an understanding of the supplies and other expenses she'll need to include in her budget. Let her make a list of expenses and calculate the total. Then review her budget together to make sure she included everything. Budget items are meant to remain static, but occasionally there are emergency expenses. Help her understand the difference between an emergency expense and a trivial one. Teach her how to allow room in her budget to accommodate emergencies.

Document everything. You never know when you need a detailed written account to prove something. In her project journal (preferably a digital one so the information is accessible from any device), your girl should be taking notes to record data on every aspect of her project: her budget guidelines, calendar adjustments, supply needs, research anomalies, experiment results, contact details, etc. This is a good habit for her to learn. Plus, she'll be able to leverage her work on this project for future endeavors like college applications and/or future science projects.

Learn to write well. Regardless of the topic, good writing gives your subject the professional consideration it deserves. Almost all science fairs require a research report as part of the competition requirements. The report might be the most comprehensive report your girl has written so far.

> *According to the article "The Importance of Writing Skills for Children," "This writing workload from school only increases as the child grows older. But writing doesn't stop with school. The importance of writing skills holds true for life. The emails that we write daily are a form of written communication too. Being keen on improving writing skills—grammatically and with good vocabulary—will ensure you consistently get better at effective communication."[30]*

In addition to bolstering her writing skills, science-fair reports are a great way for her to learn how to write an abstract and a bibliography, practice her writing mechanics, and familiarize herself with the anomalies of word processors.

Don't plagiarize. The internet and AI have made it too easy to fool readers. Copying content from a Wikipedia page or AI tool and pasting it into your own content takes seconds. But you can never fool *yourself* and plagiarizing others' work defeats the purpose of the learning process. Help your girl understand the importance of citing resources in her research paper bibliography and how much work the original author put into their own project. Compare the originator's efforts to the amount of work she's committing to her project. Let her make the connection so she feels like she owns the *ah ha*! moment.

Take one step at a time. Life is not a race. Try to focus on each task individually and not worry about everything that needs completing all at once. During the project, encourage your girl to take her time.

The calendar she completed for this project should be her only motivation—not the fact that there are other competitors doing the same project and trying to do a better job.

Learn from your mistakes. Trial and error is the best way to learn. Period. Reassure her that just because she tried something and failed, it is not the end. Keep moving forward. If needed, help her figure out why the failure occurred by asking leading questions so she can figure out the solution on her own. Sometimes just talking it out leads to a discovery. Let her draw her own conclusions, adjust her approach, and try again. Repeat if necessary.

There will always be naysayers. People like to complain. It makes them feel better about themselves. Science fairs are no different. Science fair detractors like to complain about too much parent participation, unfair judges, lousy venues, inaccurate age groups, and blah blah blah. Help your girl ignore the "Debbie Downers" and focus on what she's gaining from the competition.

Communicate your ideas. People can't read your mind. Learning to articulate, *truthful* communication is a crucial skill for both business and personal relationships. Your girl will have to persuade science fair judges about the validity of her hypothesis. This can be great practice for her to articulate her ideas. To help her, have her practice communicating her thoughts to you before she has to explain it to others.

Be aware of the world around you. From food to medicine to weather, societies around the world rely more and more on science every day. It's so easy to forget the role that science plays in our everyday lives and take it for granted. Participating in a science fair is a wonderful reminder of the magic of scientific discovery and its usefulness. The scientific literacy and awareness of the world around her that your girl is grasping now will benefit her throughout her lifetime.

Prizes are just the icing. Try to stay focused on baking the cake. It's not about winning; it's about learning along the way and using your newfound knowledge for next time. Agree with you girl that science fairs can be an excellent way to earn significant prizes, including cash, scholarship funding, and sponsored trips to more significant science-related events. Then remind her that the grand prize is new knowledge. That might not sound very appealing to her now, but hopefully it will make sense eventually.

Have fun! Life is meant to be enjoyed, not endured. Encourage your girl to pick her head up every now and again, look around her, and appreciate what she has accomplished. Tell her to keep moving forward and build on what she's accomplished so far and what could potentially be in her future—Science fairs at the national level? Scholarship opportunities? More hands-on competitions?

Encourage her to keep going. This is her time to shine!

HOW TO RAISE INCLUSIVE CHILDREN

Chapter 11.
Boys

If parents can raise an entire generation of boys with a more accurate understanding of girls' potential, we can really move the gender-justice needle in a lot of areas.

The most effective way to move the needle is to ensure that the values our boys are observing at home enforce concepts like fairness and empathy, not outdated gender stereotypes.

The way you talk to your partner, divide family chores, even small things like who empties the dishwasher make lasting impressions on how your boy considers gender justice.

Yes, he's influenced by his peers, but ultimately, the values that he'll carry with him into adulthood are learned at home.

By nurturing his emotional IQ, fostering his empathy skills, explaining false gender stereotypes, providing him with positive male role models, and staying close to him as he grows, you can give your boy what he needs to become a confident, empathic person and an exceptional man.

Step 1. Create a Gender-Equal Home Environment

It's not our words that will defeat toxic masculinity; it's our actions in the home.

That sentence is the central theme of this step. If your boy learns to be fair at home while he's growing up, he'll carry those values with him his whole life.

Household responsibilities like cooking, cleaning, and taking care of others are perfect for teaching him gender fairness.

If there are two parents in his household and he only sees him mom doing the cooking and cleaning, he'll grow up believing that he doesn't need to learn.

You'd be doing him a disservice if he doesn't learn household skills now. Therefore, it's essential for you to model a fair household responsibility routine that he can learn and mimic as an adult.

Clearly, more improvement is sorely needed. The following suggestions are structured to help you cultivate a gender-equal household.

Chores

With chores, two principles are crucial for building an equitable household: 1) Children should help equally with household tasks regardless of gender; and 2) Both genders can and should help with both inside and outside chores.

First, try to keep in mind that chores are practice for adult living. If boys are allowed to continue playing video games while girls help in the kitchen, that's the model for fairness that your boy will take into his adult life.

Second, try to refrain from assigning outside chores exclusively to boys (mowing the lawn) and inside chores exclusively to girls (emptying the dishwasher).

Repeat these words as often as you can and make sure your boy hears you:

"There's no such thing as boys' work or girls' work. It's all just work."

HOW TO RAISE INCLUSIVE CHILDREN

Of course, you know your boy best. It's completely your decision to assign the amount and type of household chores based on his developmental and physical ability.

That said, here are some ideas that *defy* the typical male chore assignments:

- empty the dishwasher
- do the dishes
- make the dinner salad
- organize the grocery list
- feed the family pet(s)
- set the table
- vacuum
- sweep
- learn to use the washing machine and start a load of laundry
- fold laundry
- pick up clutter
- dust
- help care for baby and/or ailing grandparent

If your boy complains about his tasks, listen to his complaints, and ask how he would make it more equitable (without saddling you with more work or expense). Talk about it together. He needs to feel like he's part of the discussion.

Ask if he thinks he can continue with his assigned chores for another week. Hopefully, he'll agree, his complaints will wane and then disappear altogether.

If his complaints don't disappear, offer alternative chores. He needs to know that you're listening to him and willing to compromise.

Allowance

Your boy needs to know that everyone should contribute equally to household maintenance, regardless of gender, and receive the same amount of allowance.

Although there are a few signs that the gap is slowly shrinking, most data show that starting as early as childhood allowance, girls are still paid less than boys for doing the same work.

If there are special circumstances in any given week, e.g., special chores for bonus pay, sick child, conflicting family obligations, etc., try to balance-out opportunities and payments in the ensuing weeks. Otherwise, payment should always be the same, regardless of gender.

Avoid gender-biased language

Whether we're aware of it or not, our language sends messages about our expectations based on gender.

When we comment on how pretty girls look or how strong boys are, for example, we send messages about our expectations for kids based on their gender.

Watch what you say and how you say it. Be aware that kids pick up not just the words, but the subtext of the words.

Sexist jokes, gentle jabs about a woman's weight, a boy who is emotional, sensitivity expressed as a girl thing, a boy who is considered a sissy because he expresses fear—all of these verbal subtleties are retained and absorbed more than we realize.

These kinds of female-based barbs assume a weakness in girls and women that is unfair, unkind, and simply untrue.

Yet these phrases are so ubiquitous and have been around so long, many people don't even consider their potency.

For everyday conversations, try to use words that are gender neutral. For example, the words policeman and stewardess are gender-specific job titles; the corresponding gender-neutral terms are police officer and flight attendant.

Phrases like "man up," "mankind," and "drama queen" are also deeply embedded in our daily language. We all do it.

And our kids are listening.

Because we're blind to some of our biases, we all need feedback. Talk to close friends and family members about your own gender-biased language and ask them to call you on it.

Ask your boy to hold you accountable and give you feedback if you are modeling stereotypes or expressing bias with words.

If you're grateful for his input and admit to your own bias, it will send a powerful message to him about how important gender equality is.

Once he makes it his job to correct any biased language you're using, he'll most likely adjust his own language too.

As boys grow into men, they transfer misconceptions about being a girl/woman onto the women they work with, fall in love with, and get married to.

Try to remove these misconceptions from your family's daily language so they don't get passed onto the next generation.

Note: You can search online for "gender-biased word examples" if you want to learn more.

Model gender-equal household behavior

In an ideal world, both parents (if there are two) should be doing an equal amount of housework and both parents should be contributing the same amount of work hours outside the home.

But we don't live in an ideal world, and families come in all shapes and sizes, so the 50/50 scenario is a great goal, but not always realistic. Whatever division of labor you and your partner can contribute towards the ideal 50/50 scenario is best.

If the work in the house is divided along traditional gender roles with the father doing certain "male" jobs of repairs and maintenance, and the mother doing the "female" chores of cooking and cleaning, this is what your boy will pick up and carry with him into adulthood.

Keep in mind that it's the little things that make the biggest impression. Adjust where necessary:

- Who drives on family outings?
- Who pays at restaurants?
- Who contributes to household income?
- Who goes to parent/teacher conferences?
- Who chaperones field trips?
- Who does the family laundry?

In addition to the little things, try to be a role model for having a positive attitude toward gender-equality in the media.

For example, while you're watching a show together, make a remark about how fair or unfair a certain scene is. Then talk about how it used to be accepted that men were superior to women, but that mindset is thankfully changing. Make sure your boy is listening.

Step 2. Help Him Cultivate Empathy

Empathy is the ability to understand and be sensitive to other people's feelings by putting yourself (figuratively) in someone else's shoes. It's an essential building block for learning how to treat people fairly.

When boys can understand how someone else feels, it makes them better friends now and better husbands and dads in the future—empathetic men are more likely to be tuned in to the needs of women.

The goal of this step is to provide some ideas for helping your boy develop a strong sense of empathy.

Model compassionate behavior

Just like all the values we try to teach our children, the best way for your boy to learn empathy is by following your example. If he sees you being understanding and proactive in a situation where someone needs help, odds are he'll do the same thing.

> The article "Modeling Empath for Children" explains, "While we can teach manners, empathy is something that can be modeled and practiced but not taught."[31]

Here are some ideas for proactively modeling empathy:

- Take him with you to donate winter coats. Let him help load/unload the items from the car. If the situation is right, take a moment to express sympathy for people who don't have a warm coat.

- If you see an elderly person looking for their car in a parking lot, ask that person if they need help. Make sure your boy hears and sees you helping.

- Suppose your server brings you the wrong order at a restaurant. When your boy is listening, make a point of telling your server that everyone makes mistakes, it's no big deal, and you're sure he/she will get it right next time.

- When someone is right behind you in a checkout line with only a few items and your cart is full, offer to let that person go in front of you. Make sure your boy is watching.

- If you both see a dog who looks lost and scared, with your boy, take the time to help the dog. If that means getting it into your car, reading tags and making a phone call (if it has tags), or taking it to the vet to read an identity chip, do it. Even if you have to miss an appointment/errand of your own to help the dog, it will make a lasting impression on your boy.

- If there's a particularly heart-wrenching scene on a television series or movie you're watching together, make sure he sees the tears in your eyes or hears you comment on how hard it must be for the person or animal who is suffering. If he asks questions, be sure to take the time to answer thoroughly.

HOW TO RAISE INCLUSIVE CHILDREN

- Help him discover what he has in common with other people. Helping your boy understand that all humans are basically the same is a great way to encourage empathy. One way to encourage this type of thinking is to point out people from different countries as you are out together. Have him come up with similar characteristics to his own and then talk about the similarities that he came up with.

- Empathize with him so he knows what it feels like. Here are some examples: tuning in to his physical and emotional needs, understanding and respecting his individual personality, taking a genuine interest in his life, and guiding him toward activities that reflect an understanding of the kind of person he is and what he enjoys.

- Don't be afraid to apologize (to him or anyone else). Apologizing is not a sign of weakness, but a brave act of courage and strength. He needs to know this.

- Show excitement and/or happiness for a friend who has good news.

- Hold the door open for someone who has their arms full. Make sure he's watching.

- If you both pass a homeless person on the street, talk about what it might be like to have to sleep out in the open, or not know if/when you can eat your next meal, or not have anywhere to put your stuff. Express genuine curiosity about how that person got to such a low point in their life.

Provide opportunities for him to learn hands-on "helping" skills

Your boy was born with the capacity for empathy, but it needs to be nurtured. Just like learning a second language, it requires practice and guidance. Hands-on learning is highly effective.

Regularly considering other people's perspectives and circumstances helps make empathy a natural reflex and, through trial and error, will help your boy get better at tuning into others' feelings and perspectives.

Here are some ideas for offering hands-on learning opportunities so he can practice feeling empathy:

- **CPR.** Learning CPR is a wonderful way for your boy to feel good about helping others in need. In-person classes are better for teaching compassion than taking an online certification course.

- **Animal shelters.** For information about volunteering at an animal shelter in your community, talk to local pet shop owners and/or veterinary office workers.

- **Community service.** Do an online search for community service opportunities in your area.

- **Tutoring.** If he's able, encourage him to tutor other kids who need help with their schoolwork.

Suggest (subtly) empathy-building activities he can do at home

This tip provides ideas for empathy-building activities he can do *at home* (instead of making you drive him places).

- **Superheroes.** Ask him if he has a superhero. Whoever his hero is, ask him what kind of compassionate traits this hero has. Does his hero stand up to bullies? Help the less fortunate? Support his peers by not being a bystander? Without putting him on the spot, ask him to recount an episode where his hero did something compassionate.

- **Thank you note.** Kids love this one (kidding!). Help him write a genuine thank you note for a gift he received. Not the standard "thank you for..." but something that really describes how he felt when he realized the gift matched his interests. Have him think about how the gift giver knew he would like the gift. Doing this will hopefully help him make a connection between his own feelings and the feelings of the person who gave him the gift. This is a great step towards being able to put himself in others' shoes.

- **Random scenarios.** Make up random scenarios from his world and tell him how *you* would react. Putting the onus on you to react compassionately will prevent making him feel like he's on the spot to come up with the right answer. You can sprinkle these types of scenarios into whatever timing feels right.

- **Stand up for others.** Bullying and harassment is something that boys routinely grow up with. If approached correctly, it can be a valuable teaching tool. Too often, the bully thinks of it as a game rather than as something that would have serious repercussions for the one being bullied. Teach your boy that he should stand up for anyone who is being targeted and victimized. Boy or girl. Teach him that it is much stronger to stand up for what is right than to ignore what's wrong.

Be consistent

The best way to make sure the importance of compassion is clear to your boy is to make it a consistent priority. Here are some easy ways to maintain consistency:

- Make caring for others a daily priority and set high ethical expectations. If you want your boy to value others' perspectives and show compassion for them, it's crucial that he hears it from you, repeatedly.

- Reiterate that learning to care for others is a fundamental part of growing up. Keep repeating the same message with the same words. Most parents know that teaching values to children requires repeating the same thing over and over again. Your message will sink in eventually. Even if he makes fun of you, keep saying it.

- Recognize your boy's kindness. If you witness him doing something kind for someone, comment on it, and make sure he really hears you. Make a big deal out of it, but don't overdo it. It's important that he considers your praise genuine.

- Regularly encourage him to recognize how he feels and show it, whether the feeling is good or bad. Talk with him about what may be making him feel that way. Learning about his own feelings will help him connect with others, and hopefully develop into a caring, sensitive man.

- Try to stay connected to his ability to empathize as much as possible. Make it a part of your parenting routine as he grows into himself.

Step 3. Let Him Be Himself

Too many boys are pressured to disconnect from their emotions. They get the same erroneous message about bravery from the media, their peer group, and even the adults in their lives.

This can have very harmful effects when they become adults. It can lead to things like objectifying women and resolving conflict with violence.

Instead, if we enable boys to be themselves and connect with their emotions, they have a much better chance of growing into caring, honorable men.

The goal of this step is to help you find ways to encourage your boy to be proud of who he is. Whether he naturally gravitates toward trucks or dolls is irrelevant.

Let him play with either one so he can explore who he is without becoming who he thinks you (or anyone else) wants him to be.

Examine your own judgments

One of the hardest things we have to do as parents is to look at ourselves objectively to make sure we actually believe the stuff we're telling our kids.

Really believing in gender equality means that you think men and women should have equal access to the exact same resources and opportunities, regardless of gender. Ask yourself if you truly want your boy to grow into a man who advocates for this notion.

If you're sure about your conviction, fantastic. Keep in mind though that, depending on his developmental level, your boy might have the ability to track (and dispute) the accuracy of your past statements. Just a heads up.

Keep educating yourself. Be vigilant. He'll hear lots of differing opinions from outside sources. Keep taking stock of what you believe and hammering away at the values you want him to hear consistently as he grows.

Allow him to have a full range of emotions

Requiring boys to differentiate between what they show the world and what they actually feel inside themselves happens really young. A boy grows into that mask to the point where the mask becomes how he thinks of himself.

Boys who sever ties with their own feelings are less perceptive about what they're actually feeling. They don't know how to behave fairly in a relationship.

Instead, teach your boy that it's possible to be strong *and* sensitive—the two attributes are not mutually exclusive. Keep your explanations simple so there is a better chance he'll remember what you say.

Here are some ideas for guiding him:

- **Talk extensively about emotions.** Show your boy that emotions are for everyone and that it's important to be able to feel all of your feelings in order to let go of them and move on. Point out emotions in a really practical, basic way (happy, sad) and support him through the hard ones (grief, jealousy).

HOW TO RAISE INCLUSIVE CHILDREN

- **Let him cry.** Boys cry. Girls cry. Men cry. Women cry. Everyone cries. Crying is a normal human reaction to releasing grief, hurt, pain, disappointment, and even anger. Crying is what lets the emotions out and allows you to process something that's disturbing. Crying is cathartic and essential. You can let your boy know that he shouldn't be ashamed of tears and that expressing feelings doesn't mean he's weak. If possible while he's crying, explain why it's okay to cry.

- **Emotions don't go away on their own.** Tell him that if you keep emotions inside, they'll keep stacking on top of each other until eventually there's no more room on the stack, and all the emotions will burst out at once. It's much better to let each emotion out one by one when you feel it. Whether you talk about it or cry about it, it needs to come out.

- **Books.** Depending on his age, encourage him to read realistic books like *Tough Guys Have Feelings, Too* with characters like a losing wrestler and a homesick astronaut feeling sad. Books like this show boys that sad or negative feelings are normal and nothing to be embarrassed about.

- **Toys.** Let your boy play with anything he wants (within reason). The important thing is that the toy feeds his curiosity and helps him develop skills that will eventually assist him in navigating the world as he grows. Nurture his natural tendencies, whatever those may be. If that means he wants to play with toys that are traditionally associated with girls, let him. Or if he wears colors or clothing that has sometimes been stereotyped, so be it.

- **Media.** Many of our most toxic ideas about masculinity are passed down through entertainment. This is doubly troubling because the effect is that we not only receive these toxic messages, but we also enjoy getting them because of the medium. While you still have some control over the media your boy consumes, steer him away from any media that features violence, misogyny, submissive women, and/or gender-exaggerated superheroes. The less he's exposed to this harmful culture, the better.

- **Girl-power examples.** Watch a show about a strong woman together and make comments about women's abilities. Even if he protests and tries to refute your opinion, the message he's getting will click eventually when his mind gathers enough evidence. Everyone has their own tipping point for how they formulate beliefs. Talk about it more than once.

- **Inner voice.** Teach him to follow his inner voice instead of succumbing to peer pressure: A boy who learns to trust and value his own inner thoughts, can lead others. Make sure he knows that standing up for the rights of the marginalized, like girls and women, or even himself, is actually quite brave—and should be admired.

- **Choices.** Celebrate who he is by supporting his choices. Let him make small decisions like what he wears. He needs to feel like he has some control over his own life. Once you turn the choice over to him, stand back, bite your tongue, and let him make the decision (unless it's harmful to himself or others).

- **Patience.** Teaching your boy to make his own choices takes patience. We all know how long it can take a child to choose, and while he's choosing, it's easy to worry about whether or not you're doing the right thing. But nudging him one way or another, even if our intentions are good, defeats the purpose—which is to teach him to make choices based on his feelings.

- **Play.** Don't over-emphasize physical play. Parents tend to let boys play roughly because "boys will be boys." While it's fine to let your boy roughhouse, it's important to help him learn empathy by talking to him about the feelings of the children he's playing with and helping him understand how his actions affect others.

- **Little boys are sweet.** Little boys hold hands with each other, tell secrets, and their tears come as easily as their giggles. Then toxic masculinity slams down on them. Try to lessen toxic masculinity's effect by letting your boy know that he doesn't have to live up to anyone else's definition of manhood, and that whoever he is just fine with you. Tell him he is loved and accepted no matter what.

Allow friendships with girls

When boys have equal opportunity to interact with both boys *and* girls, there is less likelihood that they'll grow up thinking of girls purely on the basis of romantic or sexual partners.

Encourage your boy to cultivate diverse friendships. This will bolster his understanding that we are all just people, and that there are traits to like or dislike about a person that have nothing to do with gender.

If he develops a friendship with a girl, definitely don't call them "boyfriend and girlfriend." Boys and girls need to understand they can interact in friendly ways that have nothing to do with romance.

Here are some thoughts about how you can be supportive of his female friendships.

- **Birthday parties.** If your boy is having a birthday party, make sure the girls in his class get invites too. Explore co-ed party activities so he starts thinking about boys and girls on the same level.

- **Play dates.** Be supportive of his requests for play dates with girls. If he finds someone he connects with, celebrate it. Ask him what he likes about her. Depending on his age, whatever bond he and a girl develop most likely has nothing to do with gender.

Be wary here though—there's no need to "push" friendships with girls. Your boy will naturally gravitate toward the playmate he's comfortable with. Just be ready to be supportive either way.

Step 4. Explain Consent So He Remembers

The #1 objective of this step is to help your boy fully understand consent and remember what it means.

The approach used here is to revisit his understanding of respect, then teach the concept of boundaries, and finally, connect respect and boundaries so that consent is as easy as possible for him to *fully* comprehend.

Basically, you want him to learn that consent is the same as respect.

The underlying context of this strategy is that while your boy is young, consent can refer to anything in his world that's important to him and deserves respect from other people.

As he grows, consent can and will apply to more mature subjects like treating girls/women with respect.

The big-picture goal here is to raise a generation of boys who don't even consider non-consensual sex as an option.

Remember that it's so important to communicate the concept of consent by framing your words into a two-way conversation instead of a one-way lecture.

The more he feels like he's part of the conversation, and not being lectured, the more ownership he'll feel for the subject.

And the more ownership he feels, the likelier it is that he'll be able to fully understand and remember consent so he can apply it to scenarios in his own life as he grows.

Review basic respect *together*

Start by making him feel good about himself. Give him a compliment by saying something like:

"I know you already know what respect is. You show respect all the time. I'm proud of that. Don't think I don't notice."

Continue by saying:

"Respect includes things like saying 'please' and 'thank you.' It also includes things like holding doors for others, pulling out a chair at a dinner table, or helping someone carry a heavy load."

Let him know that these are all examples of good manners and *not* examples of helping incapable females.

The important message to convey here is that your boy shouldn't think of these acts as chivalrous, but as human decency.

Hopefully, he'll chime in and add his own examples of respect.

If not, and he looks like he's tuning out, put the conversation on hold and try approaching it a different way another time.

If he does look engaged, continue your conversation by offering more examples of respect:

"Respect is asking permission to borrow something or letting someone finish speaking even if you already know the answer."

Tailor your ideas to match activities in his life.

"Respect is not interrupting the teacher or not borrowing someone's PlayStation controller without asking."

Keep it simple. Talking about respect/consent with him on a level that he understands will greatly increase the odds that the concept sinks in.

Keep the conversation going by defining respect *together*. Try to get him to expand on your examples. Then expand on his examples so it starts (or continues) to feel like a two-way conversation.

Here are some more ideas for defining respect together:

- **Friends.** Think of someone you both know who is respectful and talk about why they would be a good friend.

- **Respect for belongings.** This is a big issue for kids. If you're having a hard time getting things started, you could try to use this subject to get a response. If you're the target of his "respect for belongings" frustration, e.g., you borrowed something from him without asking, listen attentively to his feelings, make eye contact, and tell him you'll pay more attention to the problem and work on improving. Ask him to call it out if you do it again.

- **Media.** Watch a TV show together and point out examples of respect/disrespect and why. Do the same thing when you are out doing errands together (store clerks? parking etiquette? check-out line?).

- **Games.** Ask your boy to come up with three compliments he might give to his sister (or whomever). Let him think about it before he comes up with an answer. If he can't come up with three, help him by giving hints about what she does and how it benefits who she is. For example, if you come across a female checker at the grocery store, get him to think of three admirable things about her: 1. works hard 2. kind 3. positive attitude. The goal of this game is to get him to think about girls/women in positive terms and recognize that even though everyone is different, we all deserve respect.

Try to make sure he has a good foundation for understanding respect before continuing.

Explain boundaries

Recognizing boundaries, both physical and emotional, is an important life skill that your boy should learn. Your mission is to explain the concept of boundaries so that the definition is memorable.

Depending on your boy's age and maturity level, here are some ideas/words you could use to explain boundaries:

Invisible force field. Invisible force fields are a great way of describing something that's not meant to be crossed.

> *Another article from Hey Sigmund offers more insight: "We all have a thing around us called a boundary, which is an invisible line between ourselves and other people. It's like a force field. You can't see it but it's there. Boundaries are there to protect us from the people who feel bad to be around."[32]*

If needed, look up the words "force field" online followed by whatever your boy is into. If he's into Star Trek, look up "force field Star Trek" for ideas about explaining it in relation to something that interests him.

Invading boundaries. Take the "force field" concept a step further to explain what it means to invade that boundary.

> *"Just as important as knowing that you are in charge of your own force field, you need to know that you should never try to invade someone else's force field. For example, you already know that interrupting is disrespectful. When you interrupt someone, you are invading their force field and that's not right. We don't do it because invading other people's force field (boundary) is disrespectful."[32]*

Self-respect. Now talk about the importance of respecting *other* people's force field, and what can happen if you don't.

> *"Everyone is responsible for how they treat other people, but the person you have to treat the very best is yourself. Sometimes that means listening to what other people say and respecting their feelings. Otherwise, you're not being fair to yourself because if you treat others poorly, you're likely to get treated poorly right back."[32]*

Note: Any combination of the suggested words above will help communicate how important it is to respect boundaries.

Try to remember that the best way to get your message across is to guide, not lecture. Kids learn much more efficiently when they feel like they've arrived at a decision on their own, instead of believing in something because that's what they've been told to believe.

> In "Let Children Lead," we learn "The more you hand over to the children, the more they feel in control of their learning. By giving them ownership, I find children develop a love for learning."[33]

Help him reach his own conclusions by providing "breadcrumbs" for him to follow (just like the "force field" example). Let him add his thoughts to whatever metaphor you use. Encourage his participation.

Connect respect and boundaries with consent

Now it's time to start connecting respect and boundaries with consent using an example from *his* world. This part of the process is fundamental to helping your boy fully understand consent.

You can start by giving a simple definition of the word consent.

"No means no. Silence also means no. And even maybe means no. Only yes means yes."

Note: As you're talking, try to integrate the notions of respect and boundaries and whatever metaphors you used (from previous steps) so it sounds familiar to him.

Depending on his age, you can use the question-and-answer scenario below between your boy and his fake friend Kyle as a baseline. Use your own judgement for age-appropriate examples. Change Kyle's name?

Swap PlayStation controllers with one of your boy's treasured belongings? Or maybe the whole idea of Q&A won't work at all. You know best.

In each of the following sample questions and answers (or your own version), ask your boy if consent was given. Again, depending on his age, it's completely up to you how much repetition you use to get your point across.

Q: *You* took Kyle's PlayStation controller without asking. Did *you* have consent?

A: No

Q: *You* took Kyle's PlayStation controller without asking. Kyle saw you do it, but he didn't say anything. Did *you* have consent?

A: No

Q: *You* took Kyle's PlayStation controller and asked if it was okay. Kyle said "Well I guess maybe. I'm not sure." Did you have consent?

A: No

Q: *You* took Kyle's PlayStation controller and asked if it was okay. Kyle told you that yes it was okay. Did you have consent?

A: Yes

The goal here is to get your boy to understand that the only time it was okay for him to take Kyle's PlayStation controller was when Kyle *explicitly* said yes.

Consent goes both ways. Helping him understand how consent affects *him* will make it much easier for him to apply the same principle to other people.

HOW TO RAISE INCLUSIVE CHILDREN

Q: Kyle took *your* PlayStation controller without asking. Did Kyle have consent?

A: No

Q: Kyle took *your* PlayStation controller. You saw him do it, but you didn't say anything. Did Kyle have consent?

A: No

Q: Kyle took *your* PlayStation controller and asked if it was okay. You said "Well I guess maybe. I'm not sure." Did Kyle have consent?

A: No

Q: Kyle took *your* PlayStation controller and asked if it was okay. You told him that yes it was okay. Did Kyle have consent?

A: Yes

You'll know if and when the time is right to flip the question-and-answer scenario above (or your own version):

Talk about why the answers are the same whether he or Kyle was the one giving consent.

Reiterate your simple definition of the word consent.

"No means no. Silence also means no. And even maybe means no. Only yes means yes."

Also consider that one of the times that kids listen and learn the most intensely is when they overhear conversations (on the phone or in person) between their parents and someone else.

Make a point about the importance of consent, respect, and boundaries when you're talking to someone else, and you know your son is listening.

This might sound sneaky, and it probably is, but it's also an extremely effective way to drive home your message about consent without risking losing his attention.

Model respectful behavior

One of the best ways for your boy to learn how to be respectful is by watching the most consistent authority figure in his life. Kids learn more from what you *do* than from what you *say*.

Here are some suggestions for what you can do to give him someone whom he loves and trusts (you!) to mimic:

- **Keep your cool.** Instead of yelling, *"Don't you say that to me, it's disrespectful,"* calmly respond to his misbehavior with words like *"You know we don't talk to each other like that in our family. We treat each other with respect."*

- **Practice kind and firm discipline.** Discipline means to teach or to train, not to punish. It's not about shaming him. Discipline is a lot more effective when *not* using punitive strategies. Teaching respect and using disrespectful discipline are mutually exclusive.

- **Reiterate that everyone is different.** When children's differences are accepted, they feel heard and respected. If he has a different way of doing things, respect that difference by saying things like *"I've never seen anyone do it that way before, but I like it!"* Say *"everybody's different"* every opportunity you get.

HOW TO RAISE INCLUSIVE CHILDREN

- **Don't be disrespectful of others.** Children are master observers. If you're sarcastic, dismissive, and talk behind others' backs, he'll try out that kind of behavior soon enough. If he thinks it's okay to be disrespectful of others, he'll mimic your behavior.

- **Model positive personal ethics.** Whether it's obvious or not, he's watching you. He's watching and listening to things like whether you pay your bills on time, if you help others, if you're generous with tips when the waiter/waitress does a good job, and if you participate in charitable giving.

- **Say you're sorry if you screw up.** A mature, respectful grownup accepts responsibility and apologizes when they make a mistake. Let him see and hear you apologizing if you're wrong.

- **Share your own story.** This will help him feel like you're accessible and that he has a starting point for a conversation about respect. For example, if it feels okay to him, he might say something like *"Remember when you told me xyz, well something similar happened to me and I need your opinion."*

- **Respect your partner.** If it's a two-parent household, show respect to your partner. This will go a long way towards setting an example of how two people should treat each other. Remember he's watching you.

- **Be a good listener.** Give him your undivided attention when he is speaking to you. Listening to others' opinions without retaliation is an enormous part of learning how to respect others.

- **Be trustworthy.** Don't divulge (to others) the heartfelt feelings and experiences that he shares with you; show him that you can be a trusted adult who cares deeply about his feelings.

The modeling suggestions above are extremely hard to achieve, especially when you're in the heat of the moment. But if you can at least strive to accomplish *some* of the suggestions, your boy will be better off.

It will help him define "respect" in his own head and will also help him recognize when disrespect is occurring.

Make consent an ongoing household value

Explaining consent is not a once-and-done conversation. Issues will come up all the time that he (hopefully) feels comfortable sharing with you.

Keep guiding him toward fairness and explain why each situation that he brings up is either fair or unfair.

Make consent a daily value. It can be as simple as asking, *"May I please use your comb?"* and accepting the response.

As most parents know, getting a concept to sink in with our kids needs to be repeated over and over (and over!) again. Talking about respect, boundaries, and consent repeatedly might feel like overkill to you, but it hopefully doesn't to him.

Remember though, kids are clever. When you think you're secretly slipping consent into the conversation, he might be fully aware of what you're doing. (Just a heads-up.)

The good news is that the decisions he makes as he grows through adolescence and into early adulthood will be informed by his understanding of what you teach him about respect and consent.

Step 5. Find the Right Male Role Model

A male figure in your boy's life who advocates for women can be the key to helping him grow into a gender-equality enlightened man.

If your boy is part of a traditional family structure with a mother and a father, his father is his best potential male role model. He can show your boy respect for women, teach him that girls and boys are equally worthy, and prove that boys can be vocal advocates for girls to have the same privileges they do.

If your boy does *not* live in a traditional family structure, there are hopefully males in his life who are advocates for the rights of girls and women, e.g., stepparents, extended family, coaches, family friends, teachers, neighbors, etc.

As with all suggested discussions in this guidebook, it's always best to avoid formal, sit-down, eye-to-eye conversations. Kids naturally and immediately put up defense mechanisms as soon as they think a lecture is coming their way.

Instead, try to make your conversation as casual as possible—in the car? Watching TV? Cooking dinner? Tossing a ball?

Take advantage of any situation where you get the sense that the time is right to have a reciprocal, meaningful conversation.

List positive attributes of male role models

Start by making a mental list (or written) of positive characteristics of a male role model to give your boy some ideas about what a good male role model is.

> *"Role models show young people how to live with integrity, optimism, hope, determination, and compassion. They play an essential part in a child's positive development.*[28]

As you're talking through role model attributes, try to interject some examples of how role models could enable a positive impact on gender equality. Let him expand on your examples.

Here are a few male role model characteristics you can tout:

- **Fairness** – gives girls an equal chance to participate.

- **Good listener** - doesn't interrupt, values women's perspective, looks them in the eye when they're talking.

- **Doesn't accept sexist behavior** - makes a point of including women, not just men, in *all* conversations and encourages women to express their ideas.

- **Makes himself available to support women when they need it** - sees someone treat a woman unfairly and says or does something supportive instead of ignoring it.

- **Participates in household work and parenting decisions** – consistently says no to kids' snacks before dinner so his wife/partner isn't the only one saying it.

Encourage your boy to come up with more positive male traits and gender-equality examples.

The more he feels like he understands the relationship between positive male role model attributes and gender equality, the more likely it is that he'll grow into an advocate for girl's and women's rights.

Guide him toward finding the right role model

Finding the right role model is a huge part of teaching boys about gender equality.

You've already done the hard part: explaining the significance of feminist male role models and then listing their positive characteristics. Now it's time to review your boy's options for finding the right one.

With your boy, make a list of role model options. Dad? Stepdad? Uncle? Coach? Family friend? Teacher? Neighbor? Make sure he helps make the list with you.

When it's time to make a selection (or selections), steer him toward picking someone whom he sees on a fairly regular basis. This will make it easier for him to emulate positive traits.

If that's not an option, thanks to the internet, it's now possible to emulate someone whom you can admire and learn about regularly from afar.

Most important, let him make his own decisions (within reason) so he feels some ownership over his connection to his role model.

Step 6. Convince Him That Boys Are Part of the Gender-Equality Solution

One of the goals of the slowly growing gender-equality movement is for the next generation of young men and women to grow up in a society where mutual respect, support, and a shared sense of responsibility is the norm.

To work toward making that a reality, it's crucial to engage boys in the process. But how do we do that?

One way is to convince them that gender-equality success is actually a good thing for *everybody*, not just girls. Here are some ideas:

Praise him

The best way to engage boys is with positive reinforcement.

If you lavish a boy with praise every time he stands up for a girl who's being treated unfairly, he'll keep doing it.

Eventually it will catch on and other boys around him will do it too. (One can hope!)

Make a concerted effort to praise your boy every time he says or does something to support girls' and women's rights.

Compliment him extensively when he includes girls in a traditionally male activity. Not just a quick thanks but really look him in the eyes and tell him he did the right thing, and he should be very proud of himself.

Convince him that he'll be coming out ahead

The biggest hurdle to teaching boys that gender equality is good for them too, and not just good for girls, is convincing them that they're not giving anything up.

Just the opposite in fact. They're actually *gaining* from gender equality. They'll have less work, which means they'll have more opportunities to show off their skills and finish their work sooner.

Here's an example:

HOW TO RAISE INCLUSIVE CHILDREN

Suppose your boy is really good at a math project he's working on. But only boys are allowed to participate (so wrong!).

If, however, girls were allowed to participate, half of your boy's workload would be eliminated, and he'd be able to focus on the part(s) of the project he's really interested in. Plus, the project could be finished in half the time.

Try to foster boy/girl cooperation at home. If he has a sister, encourage him to work with her on a project.

If they work well together, make a big deal out of how the cooperation between the two of them not only made the project go faster, but also improved the quality.

One last thought: Convincing boys that they're an integral part of the gender-equality solution is not a once-and-done effort.

Instead, it should be a series of ongoing, casual conversations, actions, and positive reinforcements. Make it a part of your daily parenting routine.

Now the best part. Congratulate yourself for guiding your boy toward growing into a gender equality-enlightened man!

TRISH ALLISON

Chapter 12.
Religion

The truth is that every family has their own way of celebrating religious holidays. And that's okay. Children (and adults too) shouldn't be close-minded about what other cultures believe.

> *"Kids have a lot to gain by learning about other traditions," says Kate McCarthy, professor of comparative religion at California State University Chico, and author of Interfaith Encounters in America, "a connection to other cultures and traditions, and an enriched world view as well as the chance to think about their own traditions in deeper ways. Not only that, but study after study has shown that knowing someone from a different religion reduces religious prejudice and violence."* [34]

Whether your family is strongly religious or decidedly not religious, when your kid(s) exit your front door, they're growing up in a diverse world with people who have a variety of religious beliefs and traditions.

Take time to talk to them about the benefits of having so many religions color our world. Initiate a conversation. Base it on respecting others.

Step 1. Start with the Basics

Explain your own family's religion

Before talking about *other* religions, it's important that your child understands their *own* family's religious background and/or holiday traditions.

When you broach the subject, make your child feel like you're sharing special information with them.

The goal is to help them feel pride in their own traditions first so they can relate that feeling to friends and family who worship a different religious faith.

> *"Your family's religion is part of the history of the family and is part of the fabric of the family," says Susan Bartell, Psy.D., a psychologist in New York. "But you also need to say to your child that all religions have things about them that are great, and we celebrate that because it's part of who we are and who other people are."* [35]

Does your family have any religious rituals? Traditional ones? New ones? Kids love to talk about the things their family does together. If you're not religious, discuss a holiday-related tradition.

After you've helped your child feel a sense of honor about your own family's traditions, be sure to mention that other families most likely have their own traditions that give them the same kind of warm feeling.

Continue the conversation. It's an important concept for them to understand. If they're having a hard time making the connection, keep trying.

Offer a simple definition of religious equality

After you've helped them build a mental link between your family's traditions and other families' traditions, offer a simple definition of religious equality that's easy to understand. For example:

"Religious equality means treating all people who have different religious beliefs with kindness and respect."

HOW TO RAISE INCLUSIVE CHILDREN

By providing a simple explanation, you're not only giving your child an easy-to-process definition, but you're also giving them confidence in their ability to understand a complicated subject.

Confidence is key here. You want to get them engaged in the conversation.

Another idea for keeping it simple is to talk about the common threads of all religions.

Even though the way individual religions celebrate their faith (holidays, food, clothing, music) might be different, they all share the common threads of love and helping others.

However, when discussing common threads, keep in mind that if you try to convince your child that all religions are the same without acknowledging individual differences, you're giving them a reason to distrust anything else you say about the subject.

Your child is likely quite aware that religions can be unique, so trying to convince them they're not different is a losing battle.

But do make it clear that just because someone follows a different religious faith with unique traditions, it does not make them bad. Just different.

Try to offer a personal scenario that relates to the importance of respecting others' religion.

Maybe you were talking with a friend (that your child has met) and misspoke about a certain religion without knowing it was their faith?

Describe how you felt. What did you do? Anything else you can share?

Discuss the importance of religious equality

Now that you've offered a simple definition of religious equality, it's time to talk about how important it is.

The most important concept to teach children here is that all religions are worthy of equal kindness and respect; not just the one that's the most popular.

Instead of trying to explain it all at once, you could offer building blocks of ideas by playing a game. Try to list all the various religions that are practiced around the world.

See how many you can come up with together. Here are six religions that are generally recognized as major religions worldwide: Christianity, Judaism, Islam, Hinduism, Sikhism, and Buddhism.

There are many others but for the purposes of this chapter (teaching the importance of religious equality to children), we'll focus on those six.

Then you can talk about all the traditions that each religion practices. Try to list them all and look up more together. See how many you can both come up with. Feel free to do an online search.

The more you talk about religious diversity and the traditions of each religion, the more your child will (hopefully) start to understand the importance of respecting the way that others pay homage to whatever they believe in.

Continue by offering a matter-of-fact definition that relates to someone you both know. Familiarity might help the concept of religious equality sink in permanently.

For example, you could say something like:

"You know that our next-door neighbors are Jewish right? That means they believe in a specific biblical story about God and Jesus.

They celebrate holidays differently than we do. They have their own traditions. And you also know they're good, kind, honest people, right? They've shown us that time and time again."

Wait for a reaction here. It's important to see if what you've discussed so far has sunk in.

> *A holiday article in Scholastic magazine reveals "There are no definitive guidelines for families to teach their kids about other religions, but the more positive and engaging parents can be when talking about another religion, the more likely kids will be interested and understand another person's religious experience."* [36]

If you've been *talking up* other faiths and feel like your child is starting to *get* the importance of religious freedom, bravo! Keep going.

Step 2. Experience Other Religions *Together*

Most often when kids can learn about something first-hand, it eliminates any bias or fear they might have. And if they can have a first-hand experience with someone they love and trust, even better.

The goal here is to broaden their acceptance of different religions by providing opportunities for them to experience it first-hand.

This doesn't mean you have to join a church group and maintain daily communication with its members.

But it does mean you should make an effort to experience other religious services and traditions *with* your child.

Teach them how different cultures celebrate the same holiday

Without putting them on the spot, casually ask your child if they know anyone who celebrates a holiday in a different way than your own family's tradition.

Doing this will hopefully help them feel ownership of the subject and eager to make their own mental connections.

Suppose your child knows someone who celebrates Hanukkah instead of Christmas. If so, this could be a great opportunity to talk about religious differences together.

You can ask if they know any details of the Hanukkah tradition. What day(s) is it celebrated? For how long? Traditional food? Presents? Decorations?

If your child doesn't know the answer to any of the questions, look them up together.

Also, making something fun is usually the best way to engage children in learning activities. The same concept applies to teaching them about other religious traditions.

Engage in a religious tradition that's different from your own. Let your child take part in the tradition. Talk about what the activity you choose symbolizes.

For example, if you choose lighting menorah candles for your activity, talk about how lighting eight candles symbolizes the eight nights of the holiday. You could take it further to explain why the number eight is so significant.

Look online for religious traditions. Get creative.

The goal here is to help your child learn a tradition from a different religion by integrating that tradition into a familiar activity. Help them feel like religious traditions other than their own aren't so scary.

Participate in other religious services

The best way to understand people who believe in other religions is to experience their traditions firsthand.

If your own religion allows it, and you and your children have the opportunity to celebrate a holiday with a friend or family member who practices a different faith, accept the invitation.

Kids usually love being part of any kind of celebration. It's an easy and fun way to help them see things from another perspective. Make sure your child sees/hears you being open to the idea.

Note: If you plan to attend a service at a different church, keep in mind that some services allow children to attend and some don't. Before you go, check to make sure you're abiding by church protocol.

Teach religious tradition etiquette

Kids usually blurt out the first thing that comes to mind when they don't know the proper way to react to something new.

To prevent them from saying or doing something inappropriate, teach them how to act when experiencing a new religious ritual.

For example, suppose they spend the night at a friend's house where the family holds hands and prays before every meal, something your child isn't used to.

Tell them that even though you don't do that at home, everyone is free to do anything that's traditionally practiced by their religion (as long as no one gets hurt).

Teach your child that the best thing to do in this situation is to follow the family's lead. They invited you into their home, and out of respect, it's best to engage.

If they hold hands and pray before every meal, tell your child it's okay to bow your head and hold hands too. Tell them they don't necessarily have to say anything while their head is bowed.

Also, your child needs to know that just because they're participating in someone else's religious tradition, it doesn't mean they're betraying their own religion. It just means that they're respecting their friend's family's beliefs.

Or maybe your child encounters someone wearing traditional religious garb, chanting, and/or dancing in the street. The best way for them to react is to show respect by watching and listening. It's that easy.

Keep repeating the word *respect*. The main point you want to get across here is that *all* religious traditions deserve respect—not just the one your family practices.

Equally important is for you to model appropriate reactions to other religious traditions. If you're with your child at the friend's house who holds hands and prays before every meal, model respect by showing your child how to engage in the family's tradition. Hold hands and bow your head.

Make sure your child is watching. Later, you can talk about why it's important.

Step 3. Learn How to Answer Questions from Kids About Religion

If your child hasn't already met someone who believes in a different religious faith, it's more than likely they will at some point. Prepare yourself. They'll no doubt have a lot of questions.

Here are some common questions and expert-backed answers:

Q: Is grandpa in heaven even though he never went to church?

A: "I hope so. Let's hope together."

Q: Can I go to church with Emma's family even if their religion is different than ours?

A: "Of course, you can. Will you tell me all about it afterwards? I'd love to learn about their traditions."

Q: Why is that man wearing a cloth on his head?

A: "A long cloth wrapped around the head like that is usually worn by men who believe in either the Muslim or Sikh faith. It's called a turban."

Q: Why is that lady hiding her face with a scarf?

A: "That's called a hijab. Some Muslim women wear a head scarf around their face. It's part of their religion."

Q: Who created God?

A: "No one created God. He's always been living."

Q: Do animals go to heaven?

A: "Our pets feel like they're part of our family. I hope they go to heaven—let's hope together."

Q: Do I have to be nice to everyone?

A: "Yes. We should respect and be kind to everyone."

Q: What should I do if someone doesn't believe in God?

A: "Nothing. Everyone is free to believe or not believe whatever they want as long as they're not hurting anyone."

Q: Why do religious families have so many children?

A: "Mostly because of the support women get from their religious communities."

Depending on the age of your child, you might get some entertaining questions like:

"Why did God make mosquitoes?"

or

"Can God read our minds?"

Just like the best response to *all* questions from kids (after you're finished concealing your laughter), take their religious question seriously. It's probably a serious issue to them or they wouldn't be asking.

Follow up!

If your child has follow-up questions to any of your answers, let them know, repeatedly, that they can come to you anytime. If you don't know the answer, be honest and suggest that you look up the answer *together*.

If it's important to them, it's important to you. Look them in the eyes when you say this.

HOW TO RAISE INCLUSIVE CHILDREN

Keep the conversation going as the weeks unfold after your child asks a question or comes to you with a concern.

Discussing religious equality is not a formal, once-and-done conversation. Encourage your child to keep asking questions.

TRISH ALLISON

Chapter 13.
Older People

Instead of focusing on ageist stereotypes, the emphasis of this chapter is to help your child forge (or strengthen) a positive relationship with an older person.

We filled this chapter with practical tips and ideas, so you can send your child out into the world equipped with the skills needed to treat older people with the kindness and respect they deserve.

Each section offers tips for explaining aging basics, encouraging friendships with older people, and questions your child can ask an older person.

While there's no one-size-fits-all approach for teaching kids understanding and respect for older people, this chapter provides suggestions for scenarios that you can tailor to fit your own situation.

Every family has their own way of doing things. We get that.

Step 1. Start with the Basics

Explain aging

The most important thing to remember in this section is to keep everything simple.

Kids' opinions about aging are usually pretty simple. Try to keep your words and actions simple too.

If your child comes to you with questions after you've explained the basics, of course answer them directly and honestly. But for now, keep your initial discussion simple.

Here are some ideas and suggestions for explaining the basics of aging.

Aging is normal. Kids often think that older people have always been old. They need to hear and see that *every* old person used to be young. You could use a clock to illustrate that time always moves forward, and every day that passes means that you're aging a little bit. Aging is perfectly normal.

Everyone's health changes differently as they age. Kids need to know that some people age differently than others. Sometimes it's because of their family health history, sometimes they have chronic health problems, sometimes it's because of their lifestyle, and sometimes it's because of what they've experienced in their life.

The main point you want to get across here is that some people have health difficulties that can cause them to experience more aging problems than others. That doesn't mean those people are flawed, they're just different.

Sometimes this is a tough one for kids to grasp because as young people, they usually have zero age-related health issues.

Age-related symptoms are often unpleasant. Tread lightly here. The goal is to help your child better understand the mental and physical challenges most older people face. But there's a fine line between emulating symptoms and making fun of someone.

Here are some ideas for simulating age-related limitations. Prompt your child to describe what they're feeling:

- Vision - smear glasses with Vaseline

HOW TO RAISE INCLUSIVE CHILDREN

- Arthritis - try to pick something up with two fingers.

- Hearing - put cotton balls in your ears and try to listen to (and participate in) a conversation.

- Memory – try to remember what you had for breakfast on Thursday two weeks ago.

Lots of older people have to move from their homes. Explain that sometimes it's too hard for older people to maintain a large house (yardwork, cleaning, etc.).

In fact, if the older person is moving to a retirement community, sometimes there are fun activities like ping pong and swimming that your child might not have been able to enjoy at that person's former home.

Reassure your child that they can still visit even though that older person is moving.

Getting older doesn't mean you can't have fun. You can teach your child that just because they'll get older, it doesn't mean they have to stop having fun.

There might be limitations, but there are *always* ways to adapt.

For example, if your child likes writing or drawing or swimming, you can still do all those things when you get old. One of the best ways to get this point across is to encourage your child to do their favorite activity with an older person.

(**Note**: tailor this concept to your child's tastes and the older person's abilities.)

Once you feel like your child understands the basics of aging, it's a good time to use photographs to illustrate what you just explained.

Use photographs to clarify the aging process

One of the better ways to explain aging to a child is by looking at old photographs together.

Thinking in pictures rather than words helps learners remember because our brains can store images in long-term memory more efficiently than words.

Visuals break down information into manageable pieces that are easier to absorb.

Let's apply that concept to helping your child learn the truth about the aging process. Since kids usually think that older people have always been old, share photos of when your own parents were younger.

Or you could show them pictures of themselves when they were babies compared to now. Or share pictures of you from when you were a child until now.

Whatever pictures you decide on, while you're looking at the pictures *together*, make a point of repeating that everyone, no exception, starts out young and gradually ages as they progress through life.

It's not a bad thing; it's just how life works.

Explain that older people know more

Let's end this step on a positive note.

One of the advantages of aging is that you know more. Whether someone's had a life of hard knocks that continually teaches lessons the hard way, or someone's life has been fairly easy, and they learned life lessons from others, there's no way to avoid knowing more as you age.

Reassure your child that, yes, with age comes wisdom.

Older people might not be able to navigate the latest digital gadget, but because they've likely "seen it all," most older people can tell you pretty accurately what usually happens next in any given situation.

That makes them a wonderful resource for asking about life experiences.

Morgan Freeman tells us:

> *"Funny thing about getting older: Your eyesight starts getting weaker but your ability to see through people's bullshit gets much better."*

That's kind of a crude way of saying "with age comes wisdom," but you get the point.

Step 2. Encourage a Relationship Between Your Child and an Older Person

Children can benefit enormously from interacting with an older person. The trick is to make an older person part of your child's life, subtly and consistently.

Try to remember that your child is most likely still learning to socialize with *peers*, let alone interact with older people.

The best way to teach them how to interact is to consistently put them in situations where they can practice.

Learn the benefits of interacting with older people

First, here are some advantages from a parent's perspective:

- **Become sensitive to the needs of others.** Interacting with an older person is a great opportunity for your child to tune in to the feelings of others (empathy!). Sadly, older people are too often ignored or not taken seriously. But when you take time to get to know them, it's usually pretty easy for kids to see that seniors are just regular people with physical limitations.

- **Learn to listen well.** Here's a great opportunity for kids to learn attentive listening, a skill that will benefit them throughout their lives. Because most older people take longer to communicate a thought, it's great practice for kids to learn how to be patient, really listen and learn from the speaker's thoughts, and wait for others to finish speaking before reacting.

- **Gain wisdom that prepares them for life.** Life is full of twists and turns that nobody expects—if only we had a crystal ball that could tell us what's coming next. Older people aren't like crystal balls, but they *do* have a lot more life experience than most of us. It would be a huge advantage for your child if they could learn some of the insight that comes from living a long time and then apply that wisdom to their own lives.

Now let's look at a list of benefits from a kid's perspective:

- **Learn a new talent.** You never know when a senior has a hidden skill they've never talked about and would be willing to teach. Woodworking? Crafts? Gardening? Writing? Sewing? Music? Drawing? Photography? Cooking? It could be anything you think your child would be interested in learning.

- **Hear family stories.** What kid doesn't want to hear "dirt" about their parents when they were growing up? It doesn't even have to be scandalous—any tidbit of information about the childhood of the adult(s) in their lives seems to immediately capture kids' attention.

- **Talk to someone patient.** Sometimes parents are too busy with their own lives to sit down and have a meaningful conversation with a child (not a judgment, just a fact!). But older people not only have the time to listen attentively, but they also have the life experience to help your child make important decisions.

In addition to the benefits listed above, in general, encouraging kids to have a solid relationship with an older person while they're young helps them have positive opinions of older people when they themselves grow into older adults.

In an article titled "Benefits of Seniors and Young Children Spending Time Together" the author agrees with this thinking "...by making the effort when they are young, we are also more likely to see the same in them toward the elderly when they get older." [37]

Let's put words into practice.

Purposely schedule time with an older person

As mentioned, the best way for kids to interact successfully with older people is for you to (subtly) provide as many opportunities as possible for them to practice.

It doesn't always have to be a dinner invitation. Try to think of something an older person could help you or your child with, so your child can witness the usefulness of older people. Here are some ideas:

- Homework project
- Holiday decorating
- Help with a newborn
- Errand(s)
- Babysitting
- Purposely let your child see you asking an older person for advice

Please note: Lots of people think about including older people in holiday traditions. And that's great, but to be the most valuable, try to include older people in your child's life throughout the entire year.

Strengthening existing relationships

Here are some ideas for bolstering the relationship your child already has with an older person.

Help with technology. Encourage your child to help an older person with an internet or digital gadget problem. Not only will your child be solving a frustration for an older person (always a plus!), they'll also be building confidence in *their* part of the relationship.

Relationships need to work both ways to thrive, and modern technology provides the perfect opportunity for young and old to interact.

Common interests. Maybe your child is into baking and grandma is too? If so, schedule some time for your child to take cooking supplies to grandma's and let grandma teach them how to bake. Allow as much time as needed for them to bond.

Or maybe your child and their grandparents are fans of the same sports team? If so, make a point of scheduling a time when they can watch a game together and root for their favorite team.

Play together. Think of some ways your child and an older adult can be silly together, such as blowing bubbles, playing hide and seek or Candyland or even video games. Not only is play a vital part of a child's development and confidence, but it will also prove to your child that older adults can have fun too.

Step 3. Suggest Questions Your Child Can Ask an Older Person

It's so important for kids to ask questions because that's how they learn. The right answer to their question helps them develop a deeper understanding of something they're interested in.

Apply that concept to the importance of helping kids ask questions of an older person. The right questions and answers will lead your child to explore a deeper understanding of the value of older people.

This step explains the benefits of asking questions of older people and then provides sample questions along with the benefits for your child.

Learn the benefits of kids asking older people questions

First, let's go over the specific benefits.

Real heroes. Kids need to know that there are real heroes in the world, not comic book heroes or movie stars, but real heroes. Lots of older people have had daring experiences in their past that they don't often talk about. But if they're asked the right question, they might be willing to share.

> **Benefit:** Discovering that someone they know is a real-life hero can be a huge boost to your child's self-esteem.

Life experience. Seniors can often provide a different perspective on current events and life lessons because they've already lived through historical moments. Encourage your child to ask questions that prompt an older person to explain what happened to them, how it affected their views on life, and what they learned from it.

> **Benefit:** Learning life skills at a young age can be an enormous advantage for your child.

Patience. Life moves at an incredibly fast pace and parents, understandably, don't always have time to answer questions from curious kids. But many seniors can give a child their full attention and can also be great listeners.

> **Benefit**: Again, your child's self-confidence will benefit the most here because they'll feel like they're worthy enough to capture someone's full attention.

Now let's get into the questions themselves.

Suggest some of these questions to your child

These questions are not arranged in any particular order. Feel free to cherry-pick the ones you think would work best for your family.

Each question is followed by insight about why the question is beneficial for kids.

HOW TO RAISE INCLUSIVE CHILDREN

To help your child remember the questions you pick, maybe you can write the questions down for them.

Or maybe if you only pick two or three, they can remember the questions themselves?

It's totally up to you. Just give them a few ideas for how to remember the questions and let them pick which one works best for them.

Remember, the goal of these questions is to help your child create (or strengthen) a connection with an older person.

Here are the questions:

Q: Did you have any great pets?

> This question is a good one to start with because most people love to talk about their pets! Lots of older people have rich memories that they associate with their favorite pet and would welcome the chance to talk about it.
>
> And kids usually love to hear about it!

Q: Where did you grow up?

> This one helps give kids context as to where the older person came from. Learning about people from another state (or country) is always good practice for kids to learn more about geography.
>
> It can also be an introduction to a more in-depth discussion about how the older person ended up where they did.

Q: Do you have a favorite memory about your parents/siblings?

Here's an opportunity for your child to learn about what mattered to the older person when they were young. Maybe they had a brother who protected them? Maybe they remember a particular birthday party?

Whatever their answer is, hopefully your child will be able to feel an emotional connection by comparing the answer to family members in their own life.

Q: What summer jobs or household chores did you have as a child?

Household chores are a big deal to kids so this one could be a great way to form a link around family values. Most kids haven't ever thought of older people having to do chores when they were their age.

Your child could potentially respond to the older person with the chores *they're* tasked with. This could lead to a wonderful back-and-forth conversation about work ethics and fairness.

Q: Did you play sports? What was your favorite sport both to play and to watch?

Here's a chance for your child to envision the older person in their prime. This is super important to drive home your point that older people weren't always old.

It seems logical to adults, but lots of kids need a "visual" to fully understand this concept.

Q: What was your favorite family vacation?

Here's an opportunity for your child to learn details about another location. For example, suppose the older person says when they were young, their family traveled to San Francisco's Treasure Island to see the state fair.

Your child could ask follow-up questions about San Francisco. How was the food? Weather? Architecture? This could be a great learning experience for your child while simultaneously envisioning the older person as a young person vacationing with their own parents.

Q: Did you go to college or a trade school?

Most grade-school kids haven't even *started* thinking about their own career yet, but this question could shed some light on how careers get started.

If the older person had a passion in their teen years that they knew they wanted to pursue, this kind of discussion could lead to a great mentor/mentee-type of relationship.

Q: What type of work did you do?

This question is gender reliant. As professional opportunities for women have evolved, historically, most women were either secretaries, nurses, waitresses, or teachers.

Keep this in mind if this is a question you want your child to ask an older woman.

Q: How did you meet your spouse/partner? Describe your first date.

This question is mostly to motivate bonding between the older person and your child. Most kids always love to hear details about a love story, especially when it's being told by someone they know.

The other advantage of asking a question like this is that your child will be able to envision the older person when they were young and in love (and human!).

Q: Where was your first home and what was it like?

Here's one that most kids can (hopefully) relate to because their home is such a big part of their life.

Listening to an older person talk about their home life when they were young will hopefully give your child a warm and fuzzy way to forge a long-lasting relationship.

Q: What's your favorite movie and why?

Hopefully, if you pick this question to suggest to your child, the older person will answer with a movie that your child has heard of. If so, great.

If not, maybe they can watch it together. Or they could even make popcorn together to munch on as they watch.

Q: What are you the proudest of and why?

If the question is for a grandparent, hopefully they'll respond by saying that they're most proud of their grandchild (the one asking the question).

Your child might act like it's not a big deal to them. But most likely, it's a *really* big deal and a huge boost to their self-confidence.

Q: What advice do you have based on your life experience?

Here's a question where an older person could really grow tall in the eyes of your child. Lots of people who've lived a long time know things about life that most kids have never even thought of.

If the older person answers this question with something that resonates with your child, this is a great way for them to comprehend how valuable older people are.

Q: Who has influenced you the most?

If the older person's answer is "my parents," this question could definitely be in your favor. Most grade-school kids still revere their parents, but the tween and teenage years are just ahead.

So, if your child hears an older person say how influential their parents were, it could lay the foundation for slightly less turbulent teenage years. Just a thought.

Q: If you could go back to any age, what would it be?

Here's a fun question that allows your child to see the human side of the older person. Whatever their answer is, it will most likely include the reason why.

This will give your child a glimpse into the thinking process of an older person, while also giving them a reason to be excited about their own future.

Follow up

Without putting them on the spot, ask your child how the older person answered the question about their favorite pet. Did they say why that pet was their favorite?

Try to (subtly) draw a connection (if there is one) between the older person's favorite pet and their current life.

For example, maybe their favorite pet was a cat who loved them unconditionally after their spouse died. Point out to your child that pets often provide comfort to someone grieving a lost spouse.

The point of doing this is to further strengthen the bond between your child and the older person.

If you can help your child see the reasoning behind having a loving pet after a spouse dies, you'll be adding more context to the older person's humanity.

Finally, once your child has cultivated a relationship centered on kindness with a familiar older person (grandparent, friend, neighbor, etc.), the higher the likelihood that they'll use those same kindness skills when they meet older people as an adult.

HOW TO RAISE INCLUSIVE CHILDREN

Chapter 14.
Indigenous Americans

The truth about the Indigenous American experience is an integral part of United States history and should therefore be explained to children honestly.

But instead of confusing your child with mixed messages about the "discovery" of America or what actually happened at Plymouth Rock and beyond, we intentionally wrote this chapter to highlight the humanity aspect of the Indigenous American experience.

We hope that by the end of this chapter, we'll have shown you how to subtly plant seeds of information in your child that will lead them to question the injustice of the Indigenous American experience.

Step 1. Start with the Basics

Most children don't want complicated, gory details; they just want a simple explanation about what happened, and that is all.

That said, our approach in this step is to use simple kid logic: Who are Indigenous Americans and why does it matter? Who was here first, indigenous people or the pilgrims? And why were indigenous people sent to live on separate patches of land, especially if they were here first?

What is an Indigenous American?

Try to keep it simple while simultaneously painting an accurate picture of Indigenous Americans' history.

You could say something like:

"Imagine North America a very long time ago, before there were any major cities or roads. Numerous ethnic groups known as Native Americans called that place home. With their own languages, customs, and legends, each group was like a particular family. While some lived by the sea and fished, others farmed the land and grew corn and beans, and yet others lived in forests and hunted animals.

In addition to having wonderful customs like storytelling, amazing artwork, and unique ceremonies that honored their communities and the wider world, they were also deeply connected to nature and showed respect for the land and animals."

Of course, you can tailor the wording above to fit your child's level of development.

Who was here first?

If you tell your child that Indigenous Americans were already living in America when European settlers arrived on the Mayflower, that's all they want to know.

To them, that means that Indigenous Americans were in America first and therefore deserve all the advantages that come along with being first.

Things like feeling important, making decisions for others, and getting to pick first—everything that's supposed to be reserved for the ones who came first.

As you probably already know, that didn't happen. Gently explain that Indigenous Americans were forced from their land by European settlers.

To use kid logic for explaining this, you could tell them a story (fictional or otherwise) about a family that was displaced from their home because a group of developers wanted to build a new mall (or whatever).

Ask them questions about the developers' choices and the families' reactions. Encourage them to share their opinions about what's right and what's wrong with the situation.

The goal here is to get them thinking about the unfairness of Indigenous Americans' displacement from their land, without actually saying the words.

Here's another idea for covertly inspiring your child to consider an Indigenous American moral issue. Tell them you have a friend named James who's fiercely protective of the environment.

Everything he does (drives an EV, recycles, uses LED light bulbs, grows his own food, etc.) is directly related to using as few of the earth's resources as possible.

After five years of renting his house, James' landlord removes his backyard food garden and replaces it with a water-guzzling green lawn.

Like James, Indigenous Americans are extremely conscientious about their impact on the environment.

The goal for this example is for your child to relate James' situation to the unfairness of indigenous Americans' protection of natural resources vs. others' blatant disregard.

How it must have felt to be relocated

Now try to spark your child's empathy skills. Have them imagine what it must have felt like when Indigenous Americans were relegated to specific patches of land.

But instead of reciting dates and events of the Indigenous American territory relocation, focus on the humanity perspective by talking about families and home life.

Help your child imagine what it must have been like to be uprooted from your home.

You could say any one (or more) of the following statements:

- *"Imagine living in a place for a very, very long time, even before anyone else you know lived there. That's how it was for Indigenous Americans. They were the first people here."*

- *"Just like we have different families with special ways of doing things, there were many different 'families' called tribes. Each tribe had its own special language and traditions."*

- *"Think about how much you love your home and the park you play in. For Indigenous people, their land was their home, and they felt a deep connection to it."*

- *"Even when things were hard, they were strong and kept their traditions going. Indigenous people are still here today, and their cultures are important."*

Now let's (gently) dig into the reality of Indigenous Americans' displacement by settlers. You could say:

"People suddenly arrived and claimed ownership of the land, telling them they could only live within certain small, less desirable boundaries. This forced confinement must have felt like having your entire world shrink, cutting your ties to ancestral territories, disrupting your way of life, and creating immense feelings of loss, injustice, and powerlessness."

Consider asking your child the following question as a way to continue sparking their empathy skills:

"How does it make you feel when something unfair happens to you or your friends?"

Step 2. Explain Indigenous American Life Today

This step's approach is to focus on the resilience and adaptation skills of Indigenous Americans as they transitioned from the harsh realities of displacement from their homeland to the modern, peaceful life they live today.

They found ways to thrive and keep their culture alive. They started new communities, built homes and schools, and continued many of their traditions. They are also working to protect their rights and land in today's world, showing their strength and how they have adapted while still remembering who they are.

It's a story of great sadness but also incredible strength and survival.

Resilience and adaptation

First, lay the groundwork for the rest of this step by highlighting the strength it took for Indigenous Americans to rebuild their lives on new land.

Instead of giving up, they established new communities, often on less desirable lands, and began the difficult process of rebuilding their lives while carrying the weight of their past.

To relate this phenomenon to your child's world, think of a metaphor they're familiar with.

Maybe they had to recently relocate to a new school, or a new home, or even move a fort they built in your neighborhood.

Get into the details of how much work it is to move.

Talk about having to gather everything you want to bring with you, organize it into boxes, move the boxes to the new location, and then unpack everything so it feels familiar.

Then compare your child's moving process to what the Indigenous Americans had to go through. Emphasize that it's their positive attitude and adaptability that enables them to thrive in the modern world.

Modern life

Despite ongoing erroneous depictions of Indigenous Americans as savages, the truth is that they've grown into a thriving population of responsible, peace-loving citizens.

One way to communicate this concept is to describe the pillars of modern life they've built for themselves.

Schools. *"Imagine some groups of Indigenous Americans have their own special schools, just like yours! But in these schools, they learn cool things about their own tribes, like their special languages, stories from way back when, and how their families did things.*

They learn all the regular school stuff too, like reading and math, but they also learn what makes them special and helps them remember who they are."

Homes. *"Indigenous American tribes work together to help make sure all families have good and safe homes to live in. They help people get their own houses, fix their houses if they're broken, and even build brand new houses right there on their special tribal lands.*

Now, lots of Indigenous Americans also live in regular towns and cities. They live in all kinds of houses and apartments, just like everyone else. So, no, they don't all live in teepees anymore! That was a long, long time ago. Today, their homes look just as different and cool as everyone else's."

Culture. "Indigenous Americans' ways of life are super old and special, like really cool family traditions that have been around for many, many years! But even though they love these old ways, they also do new things too, just like you learn new games and songs.

Their special languages are like secret codes that only their families used to speak. Sometimes, other people tried to make them stop using these codes, which was not fair. But now, they are working hard to teach these languages to kids again, like fun language schools where everyone only speaks the old language!

They also make beautiful things like sparkly beadwork, cool clay pots, colorful blankets they weave, and amazing wood carvings. They still make these things, but sometimes they use new stuff and make them in new ways too!

So, their ways are old and special, but they also keep growing and changing in fun new ways!"

Business. "Think of it like this: The grown-ups in the Indigenous American tribes are like super smart business owners! They have lots of different kinds of cool jobs and businesses, both on their special tribal lands and in regular towns too!

Some of them take care of nature, like the forests and rivers, to make sure they stay healthy. Others run fun places like game centers and hotels where people can visit. They also show cool places to tourists, make clean energy from the sun and wind, create beautiful art and crafts, and even work with computers and new technology!

These businesses are like helping hands for their communities. They help people get jobs, so they can take care of their families. They also help the tribes make money to build important things like hospitals to keep people healthy and schools so kids can learn!"

...OR...use whatever language works for your child.

Step 3. Learn the Correct Answers to Kids' Questions About Indigenous Americans

While the questions and suggested simple answers below are by no means exhaustive, they'll hopefully provide a good starting point for responding to the inevitable awkward questions that kids often ask about Indigenous Americans.

Q: What's the difference between American Indian, Native American, and Indigenous American? Which one should I use?

A: "American Indians, Native Americans, and Indigenous Americans all refer to the same people. If possible, call Indigenous Americans by their tribal name, like Cherokee or Apache. Otherwise, use the term Indigenous American."

Q: Did Indigenous Americans really use smoke signals?

A: "Yes, some tribes used smoke signals a long time ago to indicate oncoming danger. But now they get their information just like us—from TV and the internet."

Q: Do Indigenous Americans still live in teepees?

A: "No, they live in houses and apartments just like us."

Q: Do Indigenous Americans still do rain dances?

HOW TO RAISE INCLUSIVE CHILDREN

A: "Yes. Some tribes have maintained the tradition to encourage crop growth."

Q: How many Indigenous Americans are there today?

A: "According to the U.S. Census Bureau, there are approximately five million Indigenous Americans in the U.S."

Q: What can I do to help Indigenous Americans?

A: "What you're doing right now is really valuable. Asking questions, learning and sharing the truth about indigenous Americans is enormously helpful. The more people that learn about the true Indigenous American experience, the more likely it is that Americans won't repeat the mistake.

By the way, it's really cool that you want to help."

Q: How did Indigenous Americans get to the U.S.?

A: "Most of the scientific evidence suggests that Indigenous Americans came from Asia in prehistoric times, either by foot over a land bridge or by using ancient boats. They were here centuries before Christopher Columbus."

Q: Which states have the largest Indigenous American population?

A: "California, Arizona, and Oklahoma."

Q: Why don't indigenous Americans like sports teams with Indian mascots?

A: "Some indigenous Americans find the concept of using humans as mascots offensive, especially when it includes racism. For example, the Washington Redskins football team name is offensive because using skin color to define an entire human population is racist and hurtful."

Q: Can indigenous Americans vote?

A: "Yes."

Q: **What's a reservation?**

A: *"When European settlers arrived in America, they wanted to reap the benefits of the new land (e.g., drill for oil, dig for gold, etc.) so they moved the indigenous Americans to patches of land called reservations."*

Q: **Do all Indigenous Americans live on reservations?**

A: *"No. More than half of indigenous Americans now live outside of Indian reservations in urban environments."*

Q: **What do modern Indian reservations look like?**

A: *"It varies. Some reservations are ultra-modern cities, and other reservations are poverty-stricken and still struggling from generations of historical mistreatment."*

Q: **What's a powwow?**

A: *"A powwow is a social gathering that honors cultural traditions like dancing and drumming."*

Q: **Why do Indigenous Americans wear feathers?**

A: *"Eagles are considered sacred, and many tribes view eagle feathers as one of the highest symbols of respect. You have to be rewarded with feathers before you can wear them."*

Q: **Why are Indigenous Americans called Indians?**

A: *"There are multiple stories, but no one knows for sure. One story is that Christopher Columbus was lost when he came to America and thought he was in the Indies."*

Q: **Do Indigenous Americans celebrate Thanksgiving?**

A: "Some do, and some don't."

Q: What kind of food do Indigenous Americans like?

A: "Traditional Indigenous Americans crops generally included corn, beans, and squash. But now they eat the same food as you and me."

Q: What's a totem pole?

A: "A totem pole is a tall sculpture, usually carved from a single tree. Totem poles were mainly carved by tribes in the Pacific Northwest and usually included numerous faces."

Q: What's a papoose?

A: "A papoose is a type of bag used to carry a child on one's back."

Q: What's Indigenous American Heritage Day?

A: "It happens the day after Thanksgiving, and it honors Indigenous Americans across the U.S. It's an opportunity for all of us to learn about past and current Indigenous American culture."

Q: What's the biggest thing that Indigenous Americans want?

A: "To be treated with the compassion and respect they deserve."

Finally, the ultimate goal of this chapter is to help you guide your child toward the DEI values (empathy, kindness, and respect for everyone) needed to respect the Indigenous American experience as an integral part of American history.

TRISH ALLISON

Chapter 15.
Disability

Whether it's because of a family member, a new friend, or a stranger, at some point your child will need to be taught how to engage properly with someone who has a disability.

The purpose of this chapter is to provide step-by-step suggestions for helping you guide your child toward the words and actions needed to treat people with disabilities respectfully.

You'll find tips for explaining disability basics (both mental and physical), cultivating a disability-inclusive environment at home, and responding appropriately to common questions from kids.

Most importantly, you want to teach your child that disability is a natural part of life. And that just like all people who are different, people with disabilities should be treated with kindness and respect.

Note to reader: We chose to use the term "disability" throughout this chapter for readability purposes only. We're fully aware that the correct terminology is "people with mental and physical differences."

Step 1. Explain Physical Disability Basics

This step focuses specifically on *physical* disabilities. You'll find suggestions for explaining physical disability basics, then discussing equality as it relates to disability, and finally, providing specific words and actions that illustrate disability acceptance.

The next step deals exclusively with *mental* disabilities, but for now, let's focus on disabilities that are visible.

Offer a simple definition

Here's a simple definition of physical disabilities that you could use.

"A physical disability makes it more difficult for a person to do certain activities or interact with the world around them."

By providing a simple explanation, you're not only giving your child an easy-to-process definition, but you're also giving them confidence in their ability to understand a complicated subject.

Confidence is key here. You want to get them involved in the conversation and feel confident about your guidance.

Do acknowledge that people who are disabled *are* a little different. If you try to convince your child that people with disabilities are exactly like everyone else, you're giving them a reason to distrust anything else you say about the subject.

Continue by offering a matter-of-fact definition that relates to someone you both know. For example, you could say something like:

"The muscles in your aunt's legs don't work like yours. That's why she uses a wheelchair."

Professional child psychologists agree with this approach.

Susan Linn, a psychologist at the Judge Baker Children's Center at Harvard Medical School, suggests that you avoid emotion or going into detail. She offers this response to a question about a person in a wheelchair: 'I imagine he may be having problems with his legs. He can't walk.'[38]

In other words, keep it simple.

Discuss disability equality

People with disabilities are human beings worthy of the same kindness and respect as everyone else. Period.

One of the better ways to get this message across is, instead of focusing on the disability itself, point out the *similarities* that people with disabilities have with other humans.

It's important that your child learns that someone with a disability is still the same in a lot of ways—they still have feelings, they like to have fun, they love their family, and they can have a favorite sport or pet.

Take care to separate the person from his or her disability by talking to your child about how they're similar.

For example, maybe your child and his neighbor who is in a wheelchair both love to watch football. Perhaps they're the same age, or maybe they both have a pet bird.

Family Education specialist Lindsay Hutton explains, "Talking about similarities will show your child that having a disability does not define a person, much like your child's physical characteristics don't define them." [39]

Another way to get the equality message across is to teach your child the words and actions needed (etiquette) to treat people with disabilities with kindness and respect.

Teach disability etiquette

There are some specific etiquette guidelines to consider when teaching children how to engage properly with people with disabilities.

Here are some things to keep in mind.

- **It's okay to notice.** People with disabilities sometimes feel insulted by those who avoid them, and your own child might get the impression that it's not okay to ask questions. Instead, if your child stares and says, *"What's wrong with that lady?",* use simple words to explain the possible reasons that person walks or communicates in a different way.

After you've explained the disability, help your child focus on the person, and not their disability. You could talk about what they're wearing or what they're eating. Anything that focuses on them as a person and *not* on their disability.

- **Keep it simple.** Kids, especially young ones, are naturally curious, so when they see someone with a disability, their first instinct is to ask about it. If you see your child staring at someone with a disability, take the lead and start a conversation, but avoid a detailed explanation or a lot of emotion when explaining it. A short and matter-of-fact description will answer your child's questions while communicating that the person has nothing to be ashamed of.

For example:

Scary Mommy's Katy Epling explains "If you see a child in a wheelchair, you can say to your own child, 'I see you looking at that little girl in the wheelchair, and you might be wondering why she needs it. Some people's muscles work a little differently, and her wheelchair helps her move around, just like your legs help you.'" [40]

- **Don't show pity.** Try to keep your emotions out of the conversation. If you say someone's disability is sad, your child might feel pity for that person. Part of teaching children about disability is to prevent them from feeling pity for people who are disabled. Mentioning your own feelings of sadness is *not* helpful.

- **Stay positive.** It's important to give your child the specific positive words they need to speak respectfully about someone who has a disability. Try to keep your explanations positive.

For example, explain that hearing aids help others hear and wheelchairs help others move around, instead of using negative statements like "he can't hear," or "she can't walk."

- **Use current terminology.** Avoid outdated, derogatory terms like "crippled," "retarded," and "handicapped."

"Let me gently suggest avoiding the words 'sick' and 'wrong'—as in, 'That boy has a sickness that makes it harder for him to talk to people,' or 'Something is wrong with her brain, so she can't talk as well as you can.'"[40]

- **Social skills.** Teaching your child how to play with children with a disability can be tricky. Here are some ideas for easing the process:

According to the article "Teaching Your Child About Peers with Special Needs," "If your child wants to have a playdate with a child with a disability or invite him or her to a birthday party, encourage it. Call the other parent and say simply, 'How can we make this work?' Even if a child doesn't talk, there are still activities the children can do together, such as play board games or arts and crafts. Share any concerns with the other parent. Parents of children with disabilities will often be happy to facilitate a successful play date or outing. Extra effort goes a long way. For instance, learning simple signs so that you can better communicate with a child who is deaf (and uses sign language) will be much appreciated."[41]

- **Ask first.** Always ask the person using a wheelchair (or any assistive device) if he or she would like assistance *before* you help. Your help may not be needed or wanted.

Wheelchair Etiquette and Disability reveals "Wheelchairs give the person a sense of mobility and allow them to take part in activities that they otherwise wouldn't be able to. This gives the person a sense of individualism. Sometimes they might not need help."[42]

- **Be kind.** Remember to keep a respectful demeanor.

"When meeting someone who uses mobility equipment for the first time, do offer to shake their hand, even if it seems they may have reduced limb movement. This is to keep social norms and also serves to acknowledge them as a person, not as their disability. If you're unsure of something, just ask the person. This includes offers of assistance with any task, from moving to eating or drinking. It will save both you and them an awkward moment, if you clarify any help they may need, before rushing in guns blazing to assist them. Give them the option to refuse your assistance and don't take offense."[39]

Physical disability vs. mental disability

As always when teaching children, it's best to keep it simple.

Here's a simple way to explain the difference between physical and mental disabilities:

"Physical disabilities affect the body while mental disabilities affect the brain."

We'll discuss mental disability in detail in the following step. But for now, all your child needs to know are the following two general concepts:

1. Mental disabilities can be just as debilitating as physical disabilities and therefore deserve the same respect.
2. When someone has a physical disability, it does not automatically mean they also have a mental disability.

Technically, mental disabilities are further categorized into intellectual disabilities (IQ, etc.) and mental illnesses (mood, etc.).

For the purpose of this chapter however (guiding your child toward disability *understanding*), the only two concepts your child needs to know are the two that are numbered above.

Step 2. Teach the Basics of Mental Differences

Mental differences can be an abstract notion and often hard to understand (especially for children). But it's worth understanding the subject and spending time to help your child understand mental differences and the role they play in our society.

The American Academy of Child and Adolescent Psychiatry tells us "When parents talk with a child about mental illness, it helps if they are knowledgeable and reasonably comfortable with the subject. Parents should have a basic understanding and answers to questions such as what mental disabilities are, who can get them, what causes them if that is known, how diagnoses are made, and what treatments are available. Some parents may have to do a little homework to be better informed." [43]

This step is intentionally structured to help you explain mental differences efficiently. First you can offer a simple definition, then explain that mental differences can be hard to detect and then discuss unusual behaviors and appropriate reactions.

Finally, tie everything together by reiterating that all people who are different, regardless of mental vs. physical disabilities, deserve kindness and respect.

Offer a simple definition of mental differences

First, it's crucial that your child feels confident that you're knowledgeable about mental differences. Start by offering a simple definition:

"Mental differences affect a person's brain, which determines how they think and act."

Wait to see how your child reacts. They're likely busy applying your words to scenarios from their own world.

If they have a question about a friend or family member with a mental difference, it's often because they're worried about safety.

Take the time to answer their questions honestly and thoroughly. Assure them that you take your job as a parent very seriously. And one of your most important jobs as a parent is to make sure they're safe and feel loved at all times.

Tell them that they can come to you anytime with a question or concern. Look them in the eyes when you say this. When it's clear they feel reassured, praise them for grasping such a complicated subject.

If your child looks like they're not understanding your definition, consider comparing mental differences to physical disabilities. You could say something like:

"Just like someone who has muscles that don't work well (some people may need to walk slowly, and others might need a wheelchair), a person with a mental difference might need a lot of help or very little. Each person is different."

There's no need to get into the details of all the different types of mental differences at this point. We'll talk about unusual behaviors associated with each type of mental difference later on in this step.

Explain that mental differences can be hard to detect

Children need to understand that just because someone isn't using a visible aid, e.g., wheelchair, white cane, stair lift, etc., doesn't mean they don't have a different mental ability.

Remind your child that millions of people, including leaders and authority figures, have a mental difference. To find examples that your child can recognize, do an online search for the phrase "famous people with mental differences."

Explain that we can never tell what someone is experiencing or has experienced in the past just by looking at them. So, the smart choice is to treat *everyone* with kindness and respect.

Let that sink in and say it again if you feel like it needs repeating.

Watch your child's reaction during this conversation and make adjustment(s) if needed.

- Do they look confused? Offer to (calmly) repeat what you just said.

- Do they look anxious? Consider toning down your rhetoric or shelving the conversation. Depending on your child's age, they might be feeling unsafe. Reassure them that mental differences aren't contagious.

- Do they look bored? Try asking them if they know someone with a mental difference that's hard to detect. Try to engage them in the conversation as much as possible. If nothing works, save it for later; they usually come back when they're ready.

Whatever they're feeling, validate their emotions. Your child needs to know that their thoughts and feelings are safe to share with you.

Teach your child about mental differences and unusual behaviors

The purpose of this section is to help your child understand why people with mental differences sometimes exhibit unusual behaviors. The #1 priority here is to teach your child to react to those behaviors with kindness instead of bullying.

In most cases, the best way to get your message across is to explain why the behavior is happening in the first place and then relate it to something from your child's world.

For example, have your child imagine a boy in their class named Justin who has a learning disability. To help your child learn how to treat Justin with kindness, explain that everyone's brain works differently, including Justin's, and that's why he takes longer to grasp certain concepts.

Tell your child that Justin doesn't purposely take longer to learn, in fact, he probably knows it makes him stand out, but he can't help it. Most important, the fact that Justin's brain works differently doesn't make it okay to be mean to him.

Here's a list of common behaviors and how to help your child understand why they're happening.

- **Fidgeting/stimming.** Fidgeting or "stimming" (shorthand for self-stimulation) is displayed in a wide array of movements. It's really individual how these "explosions of energy" are exhibited.

  How to help: Help your child understand stimming by comparing it to how energetic and uncomfortable they feel after eating too much candy, or cookies, or some other sugar-filled food. Ideally, have the conversation when they're in the midst of a sugar high. Relate that feeling to stimming.

- **Conversation issues.** Some people with mental differences interrupt, don't listen, and dominate conversations. Most often, they do this because it feels safe and soothing to them.

  How to help: Help your child understand this concept by explaining that people with conversation issues aren't doing it to be intentionally annoying. Rather, they're doing it because they don't comprehend the concept of back-and-forth conversations. Conversations, to them, are for communicating their own ideas; they're not for integrating new information and letting other people contribute their thoughts based on the new information. Monologues feel more comfortable and safer to them than back-and-forth conversations.

- **Sensory sensitivity.** Sensory sensitivity can display itself in numerous ways. It can be visual, auditory, olfactory, tactical, gustatory, or all of the above.

How to help: Help your child understand why someone reacted so strongly to certain sensations. Try to use a simple example like the sound of metal scratching on a chalkboard. If possible, physically replicate the sound. Explain that when someone with a mental difference covers their ears, it's because they're trying to soften the intensity of the sound.

- **Motor clumsiness.** Some people with mental differences are awkward at group sports. They might enjoy participating on a sports team from a mathematical perspective (i.e., baseball statistics or score keeping), or in an individual sport (i.e., martial arts or cycling) but due to lack of coordination and/or focus, participating successfully as an athlete in group sports is not common.

How to help: Help your child understand this concept by letting them talk about their thoughts on the subject. Have them tell you how someone's clumsiness affects them.

- **Hyperactivity.** People with mental differences are sometimes hyperactive. Hyperactivity is often characterized by a short attention span and/or impulsiveness.

How to help: Help your child understand this type of behavior by explaining that someone with a mental difference is hyperactive because a part of their brain works differently than other people's brains. Suppose your child tells you they have a friend who constantly wiggles. Explain to your child that they most likely do this because a part of their brain works differently, and their body responds with excessive activity. It's not intentional.

Let your child contribute to the conversation. The idea of being kind to someone who shows unusual behavior will sink in much more effectively if your child takes part in verbalizing the concept.

Encourage them to participate.

Step 3. Learn How To Answer Disability Questions from Kids

If your child hasn't already met someone with a disability, it's more than likely they will at some point. Prepare yourself. Your curious child will no doubt have a lot of questions.

The suggestions in this step are meant to help you answer the hard questions and guide your child toward being kind and respectful toward people with disabilities.

Q: Are disabilities contagious?

A: "No disabilities are not contagious. They're not like the flu or a cold that you can catch from someone else."

Q: Why do they act like that?

A: "They act like that because part of their brain is different from ours. That part of their brain is sending signals that make them act differently."

Q: Why doesn't she talk like me?

A: "She has trouble with the muscles that make it possible to talk like other people."

Q: Are they retarded or something?

A: "First, 'retarded' isn't a nice word. Please say mentally disabled instead. To answer your question, their brain functions differently, so they have a harder time talking and learning than most people. But other than that, they're just like you and me. Being a little different is actually pretty cool."

Q: Why did that happen to him?

A: "Some people are born with disabilities, and others get hurt or sick and become disabled later in life. They didn't do anything to deserve the disability. It's just a part of life."

Q: Are they going to live to be grownups?

A: "No one knows the answer to that. But doctors and scientists are working hard to find a cure so they can grow into an adult."

Q: Will they ever be able to walk?

A: "I don't know for sure, but I suspect they're working hard along with their doctors and parents to do the best they can."

Q: Are they a daddy/mommy?

A: "Yes, they could possibly be a mommy or daddy. They might have a little girl or boy at home that's just like you!"

Q: Why is that person in a wheelchair?

A: "Their body is different from ours and they need to use a wheelchair to get around. There isn't anything wrong with being different."

Q: Why can't they walk like we do?

A: "You're right. They walk differently than we do. There are lots of different medical reasons that control how someone walks."

HOW TO RAISE INCLUSIVE CHILDREN

Q: How do people take care of themselves and get around if they are blind?

A: *"People who can't see find lots of different ways to do everyday activities just like you and me."*

Q: Can they still play with us?

A: *"Yes! They might play in a different way, or they might need a little help, but they can definitely play. Let's ask them what games they like."*

Q: Can I ask them about their wheelchair/hearing aid/etc.?

A: *"It's okay to be curious, but let's be polite. You could say something like, 'That's a cool wheelchair!' If they want to tell you more, they will."*

Q: Should I be scared of them?

A: *"No way! People with disabilities are just like us. They have feelings, they like to have fun, and they want friends. There's nothing to be scared of."*

Q: How can I be a good friend to someone with a disability?

A: *"Just be yourself! Be kind, include them in your games, and ask them what they like to do."*

TRISH ALLISON

Chapter 16.
ASD Siblings

Sibling relationships play an enormous role in a child's developmental growth. Often, they are a child's first exposure to a social network and therefore, become the foundation for a lifetime of social interactions.

UNM Health Sciences says "There is evidence to suggest that healthy sibling relationships promote empathy, prosocial behavior, and academic achievement." [44]

While growing up as the sibling of someone with autism can certainly be challenging, most siblings cope very well.

Note: In the tips below, when you see the term *ASD sibling*, know that we're talking about your developmentally typical (neurotypical) child who has a brother/sister on the ASD spectrum. When you see the term *ASD child*, we're talking about your child who is on the ASD spectrum.

Tip #1. Give them age-appropriate information

It's crucial to explain ASD in age-appropriate terms.

According to child psychologist Dr. Nicole Beurkens, "Siblings don't need to know all the details, but they should have age-appropriate information about their sibling's diagnosis, needs, and anything else that is important. Hiding these things from your other kids will only cause them to make up stories in their mind that may not be true and can leave them feeling unnecessarily scared or frustrated." [45]

One of the points that your explanation could include is that, unlike a lot of disabilities, ASD is hard to detect.

You could compare ASD to a particular toy that your ASD sibling is fond of (or a book or a piece of sports equipment or whatever feels age-appropriate). Imagine together that the toy has an inner part that's connected differently than other toys.

Explain that no one would know that there's something different about the toy because it appears ordinary on the outside.

But in reality, the toy doesn't function like other toys because one of its inner parts is connected in a different way. Finish the conversation by comparing ASD with the toy that has the dissimilar part.

Tip #2. Don't be a superhero

If you're constantly fielding complaints about the way you're handling your ASD child's behavior, make it clear that you don't have all the answers.

Explain that you and the professional psychology community are trying very hard to do the right thing.

Point out that you're keeping up with all the latest information about ASD behavior. (It's good for your child to see you adapting to change.)

By admitting this, you'll be offering a more realistic view of yourself as someone who is coping and learning on a day-to-day basis. You'll also be sending the message that you are not a superhero whose achievements are unattainable for the average person.

Tip #3. Encourage appropriate participation

There's a fine line between the ASD sibling who helps during family emergencies and the ASD sibling who takes on the responsibility of a full parenting role.

Try to have an ongoing awareness of this very fuzzy line.

Here's an example. A helpful ASD sibling is the one who stands-by ready to help during a grocery store meltdown, while the parent executes a calming technique that has worked in the past.

Conversely, the ASD sibling who has taken on too much of a parenting role is the one who applies the calming technique instead of the parent.

Allowing your ASD sibling to help is positive and will hopefully empower them to embrace their own capabilities. However, enabling them to assume a full parenting role is detrimental and should be discouraged.

Tip #4. Teach them how to explain ASD quirks

At some point, your ASD sibling will find themselves in the awkward position of having to explain ASD behavior.

Provide an opportunity for your ASD sibling to practice explaining a specific behavior to you before they attempt a formal definition to others.

Their explanation might sound rudimentary to you, but it doesn't to them. After you feel like they have a basic understanding of an ASD behavior, e.g., stimming, rigid routines, sensory sensitivity, etc., let them rehearse their explanation to you again.

Practice and refine it together.

Tip #5. Justify household rules

You might find yourself constantly explaining why the rules and expectations are different for different members of your household. For example, maybe your ASD child gets to spend extra time on the computer and/or less time doing homework.

Explain to your ASD sibling why it's happening. Explain, if relevant, that their brother/sister does homework with a special teacher at school and therefore doesn't have as much to do at home.

This will hopefully dispel any claims of unfair treatment. If not, continue explaining that extra time on the computer might help their brother/sister develop the skills needed to live as independently as possible, which could benefit the whole family.

If you explain it as being an advantage for the entire family, that might allay any claims of favoritism. It might also help your ASD sibling feel like you're entrusting them with special information.

Tip #6. Reassure them that ASD isn't contagious

Sometimes kids think that ASD is contagious. It's not. You have to be born with it. If your ASD sibling has doubts, reassure them that it's not like a cold or the flu; it can't be "caught."

Tip #7. Validate feelings

Your ASD sibling needs their feelings validated all the time. It might feel like overkill to you, but it's probably not how it feels to them.

"If you're stressed out over the fifth teacher meeting in a month regarding your son's meltdowns, it's safe to say that your other child/children feel stressed out too." [45]

They need to know, repeatedly, that it's okay to feel sad or embarrassed or guilty or angry or happy or neglected, or any other feeling they might be having. Try to be aware of the multitude of feelings that they could be having and create ways for them to share with you.

Teaching by example is usually the best way to demonstrate how to share feelings. For instance, when the two of you are alone you could say something like "I'm so frustrated that your brother/sister won't wear the new clothes I bought."

Hopefully, this (or something like it) will motivate them to mimic your behavior and express their own feelings.

If not, try the same strategy again on another day or so. To open the conversation without putting them on the spot, you could use words that are as obvious as "...these are my feelings...".

Whatever works best for you and your child is the right thing to say. It's so important for them to feel like they can share their feelings without the threat of making you more frustrated or losing your love.

Tip #8. Create personal space

Your ASD sibling needs to feel entitled to their own belongings and their own private space in the world. This will hopefully reinforce the notion that they are a complete person separate from their role as an ASD sibling.

Find a spot in your home that they can call their own. It doesn't have to be big; it can even be as simple as a shelf or a drawer. Just something that is solely theirs. Make sure that both your ASD sibling and your ASD child understand the boundaries.

Tip #9. Show compassion

Try to create an environment of compassion for differences in others.

Model a positive perspective by always pointing out the constructive traits of being on the autism spectrum, e.g. enthusiastic, conscientious, unprejudiced, honest, smart, etc., instead of dwelling on the negative.

Children mimic their parents. The way that you react to the challenges of your ASD child can be an example of compassion for your family members. They will follow your lead.

Remember that your ASD sibling will have to deal with many different people, personalities, and challenges as they navigate their way through life. Learning compassion from your love and guidance will give them a head-start on succeeding in life.

Tip #10. Develop family resistance

Most families with chronic disabilities struggle through times of fear and despair. The way that you show your true colors during those tough times can be a positive learning tool for your family members.

If you can, when new challenges arise, instead of thinking to yourself "I can't take this anymore," approach the problem using the coping skills and resources you've gathered so far.

It's important for your family members to see you face new challenges with courage and determination. They will hopefully do the same.

As your family copes and learns together, the stressors of living with an ASD family member can develop into many positive coping mechanisms: family closeness, an understanding of your own strengths and limitations, resilience, and new problem-solving skills. It's not easy but try to focus on the positive.

Tip #11. Encourage participation in separate activities

ASD siblings do much better when they participate in activities separate from their ASD brother/sister. Some experts even suggest that the two children attend separate schools.

The activity that's appropriate for your ASD sibling might not be appropriate for your ASD child. And vice versa. If you encourage them to do things separately, no one will feel like they need to perform better or worse to accommodate their sibling's skill level.

For example, if your ASD sibling wants to try out for a school sports team, but is hesitant because of your ASD child's athletic limitations, encourage your ASD sibling to try out for the team.

Reassure them that you'll find an activity for your ASD child that takes place on the same day at the same time, so there won't be any hurt feelings.

Tip #12. Explain that it's nobody's fault

Watch for hints that your ASD sibling is blaming themselves for their brother/sister's impairment. If you suspect there is any doubt in their mind about the cause of ASD, reiterate that it's simply a cell mix-up at birth and that it's nobody's fault.

You can say this as a general statement; it doesn't have to be in reaction to something else. Just say it out loud, more than once, and it will hopefully sink in eventually.

Tip #13. Tell them they matter too

Your ASD sibling needs to know that they are on your radar too. Repeatedly. feeling loved and respected will make it so much easier for them to cope with the challenges of being a member of an ASD family.

Dr. Larissa Hirsch confirms, "When you have a child with special needs who needs a great deal of support and encouragement, the other children may feel that their achievements are taken for granted." [46]

One way to help ASD siblings feel valued is to spend some one-on-one time together.

For example, you could surprise them at school for a special lunch with you. A gesture like this will let them know that they matter to you too.

They need to know their actions and achievements are just as important to you as the other members of the household.

Tip #14. Share a secret code

Make it clear to your ASD sibling that they can come to you with questions and concerns anytime. Take time out to tell them that you're always willing and available to talk.

Strategize a signal together that can be used to alert each other that something's wrong when others are in the room. It could be either a specific word or gesture, just so that you use it specifically for these situations.

Sharing a "secret code" together will reconfirm to them that they're not alone.

Tip #15. Get help from outside sources

Ignore the stigmas. Counseling from a mental health professional can be a huge advantage both for you and for your ASD sibling.

A good counselor will provide knowledge about specific tools and methods. Ask someone at your children's school or your pediatrician for a recommendation.

Support groups (Facebook ASD family groups) are another great way of helping your ASD sibling feel connected and informed. Being part of a group will confirm to them that they're not the only person in the world coping with an ASD family situation.

Just having someone nod their head in agreement while you're talking can be enormously empowering.

(If you're unable to find a suitable support group in your area or online, think about starting one of your own.)

TRISH ALLISON

Chapter 17.
Cultural Diversity

The truth is that there will always be cynics of cultural diversity who believe that human diversity is something to be feared, not celebrated.

But the good news is that there are large(r) segments of our society that *embrace* cultural diversity and want to pass that appreciation onto the next generation. Infusing that forward-thinking perspective into kids' thought patterns is incredibly important.

Here's why.

Imagine you have an eight-year-old who'll be entering the workforce in 15 years (give or take). The odds are they'll be interviewing for a job with someone from Generation Z who'll be between 30 and 42 at that point.

That enlightened Gen Zer will most likely give the job to a candidate with an established progressive mindset.

That said, one of the more important parenting responsibilities *now* is to raise children who can, despite the politics of the moment, successfully grow into a society that embraces justice for all humans.

This chapter (and book!) is for those parents.

Step 1. Start with the Basics

The purpose of this step is to help your child understand, fundamentally, that there are other countries and cultures in the world besides their own. In fact, there are 195 countries in the world today, and they all have unique cultures.

A child's understanding that there are other countries in the world that are just as important as their own doesn't come naturally.

But for the purpose of this chapter (guiding them toward a sense of camaraderie with world cultures), it's a really important concept to communicate successfully.

Discuss country origins

Briefly explaining how different countries emerged during the history of our planet is a good first step for this basic discussion.

You don't have to go into details about who won what war and how countries were subsequently settled. A simple explanation of how countries were established is good enough.

All you have to say is that country boundaries were originally created either by natural features like rivers and mountains or by empires and conquests.

For example, France and Germany's boundary is marked by the River Rhine. And the Roman Empire's vast territory eventually split into several different countries.

Keep it simple. They'll likely learn more via school curricula.

This basic discussion of countries is simply to lay the foundation for specific suggestions—later in this chapter—that help your child understand that other countries with unique, beautiful cultures exist.

This could be a good time to ask your child if they know anyone from a different country. If they're not 100% sure how to answer, offer your own ideas.

If you know someone from another country that you both know, that's great. If not, talk about someone from your world.

Talk about that person's situation. Have they been in their new country a long time? Do they work? Do they have kids? How well do you know them? What kinds of traditions from their home country do they practice? Do they share their traditions with others? Are they good people?

Offer as many positive words as you can here. It's best to begin your child's understanding of the importance of different cultures with a sense of familiarity and confidence.

The odds of them wanting to learn more about other countries and their cultures will be much greater if they feel confident about the subject from the beginning.

Offer a simple discussion of the development of unique cultural traditions

Now let's bridge your previous discussion of country origins with world cultures.

You could say that each country has its own way of doing things, and that's called culture.

Culture includes things like the type of food they cook and eat, the way they worship, the language they speak, their music, the clothes they wear, and the art they create.

You might need to pause here to let that sink in. The concept of culture can be a pretty murky concept for kids to understand (depending on their age).

If they look uncertain, offer to answer any questions they might have.

Once you feel like the concept is clear, it's time to soften the concept of world culture.

Depending on your child's age, when you say the words *world culture* to kids, their minds might be filled with images of scary costumes, weird weapons, or abrupt dance moves.

The goal here is to transform that vision into something safe. The best way to do that is to associate the concept of "world culture" with something from your child's world.

You could say that culture and tradition usually come from family backgrounds.

Associating culture with family will hopefully envelop the concept in the warm, familiar feelings that family typically denotes.

Talk about your own family's heritage

To help your child feel more connected to the subject of world culture, it's important to help them understand their own family's heritage.

When you broach the subject, try to make them feel like you're sharing special information with them.

Help them feel pride in their own heritage *first* so they can then relate that feeling to people from other countries.

According to the article "Why It's Important to Teach your Kids About Genealogy," "Knowing your lineage and feeling connected to your family is always advantageous, but when you start learning as a kid the benefits seem to multiply." [47]

Kids love to learn about their family's past, and the benefits for understanding the importance of cultural diversity are enormous. Look online together to discover which country your family's ancestors originated from.

Talk about it. Make it fun.

Does your family have any customs related to your heritage? Traditional ones? New ones? Make the connection between your current family customs and your heritage.

After you've helped your child feel a sense of pride in your own family's heritage, be sure to mention that other families most likely also have their own traditions that give them a warm feeling when they experience those traditions together.

Learning about your ancestors, celebrating family traditions, embracing your culture, and understanding where you came from can really help your child make a mental connection between their own family history and the existence of other countries and cultures.

As you're discovering and discussing your family tree together, keep in mind that the goal is to help your child understand that the world is made up of lots of different families from other countries with unique cultures.

Interject as many statements as you can to validate that.

Step 2. Talk About the Importance of Cultural Diversity

Now let's discuss the most effective way to communicate the advantages of living in a world filled with so many unique and wonderful types of cultural experiences.

Our approach in this step is to first talk about the downside of uniformity, then discuss the advantages of having different options, and lastly, connect those two concepts with the importance of cultural diversity.

The reason we structured the step this way is because, from a kid's perspective, understanding how boring the world would be without variety is the best gateway to the final goal of understanding the benefits of cultural diversity.

As always, the smartest way to communicate new concepts to kids is to start with the basics to build their confidence and then work your way up to your intended message.

Imagine *together* a world where everyone is exactly the same

Begin your child's understanding of the benefits of cultural diversity by discussing *together* what everyday life would be like if everyone were exactly the same.

Make it a conversation about your child's world by walking through a typical kid's day in a world where everyone is exactly the same. Depending on what they're into, start by offering your own ideas.

If they're into food, talk about what it would be like to eat the same thing for every single meal.

Or if they're into clothes, talk about how boring it would be if everyone wore beige khakis and a white shirt every day.

Whatever you choose for your "sameness" example, the point to get across is that we need variety in our lives; otherwise, life would be incredibly dull.

Then encourage your child to contribute to the "sameness" example so they feel like they're part of the conversation.

If they need prompting, and depending on their age, you could ask about things like video games, social media, TV shows, house style and color, music, pets, type of bicycle, or family members.

When you're finished talking about what a typical kid's day in a world of sameness would look like, ask them their opinion of how it would feel to live in a world where everything's exactly the same.

Steer them toward a conclusion of how boring and monotonous it would be to do, wear, or eat the same thing every single day.

Note: An easy mistake to make here is to be too obvious that your big-picture agenda is to convey the value of cultural diversity. The worry here is that your child will consider the conversation a lecture. Instead, try to keep the discussion fun and playful, with the ultimate goal of having them arrive at a conclusion on their own.

Describe the importance of variety

The purpose here is to make a comparison between the boring sameness you discussed previously and the benefits that variety provides.

In the next section, we'll connect culture to diversity, but for now, keep the discussion about sameness and variety.

Expand on one of the scenarios you came up with previously.

For example, maybe one of the "sameness" examples you talked about was how boring it would be to eat the same pre-portioned food for every meal.

Take it a step further by discussing what those meals would consist of. Would they all be bland beige cubes of prepackaged protein?

Ask your child for examples of monotonous meals.

Pivot the conversation to the richness of variety. Have your child imagine the feeling, after a full year of bland food, of biting into a warm flavor-packed taco or savoring a piece of gooey pepperoni pizza.

Whatever scenario you expanded on from your previous discussion about sameness, make a big deal about the difference between the boring beige world and the magnificence of variety.

Connect one of their interests to cultural diversity

Now it's time to connect the importance of variety to the benefits of cultural diversity. The best way to get this connection across is to keep utilizing the same scenario from their world that you've been discussing.

Here are some ideas:

Again, if you've been talking about food, you could say *"Did you know that tacos are central to Mexican society. Traditional taco stands, or 'taquerias,' are where people gather to share flavorful, nutritious, affordable meals."*

Or if you've been talking about clothes, you could say *"Did you know people in different countries dress according to the climate in their country?*

That's why the Japanese kimono is loose-fitting and made from silk or cotton for warm Japanese weather. And the South American poncho is made of wool and is perfect for layering clothes and providing warmth in cold climates like the Peruvian Andes."

(**Note:** Whatever "did you know..." question you decide on, don't make it so bizarre that they turn off to the idea of embracing other cultures. For example, if they're into food, don't say anything about eating raw meat or live animals.)

Try to make it positive, something they'd consider appealing.

The big-picture goal is to connect one of their interests to the richness of human diversity.

By making the connection, you're laying the groundwork for your child to embrace and participate in one (or more) of the ideas in the next step.

Step 3. Integrate Cultural Diversity into Household Activities

Before we dive into answering kids' questions, let's go over the best ways to include cultural diversity in your household activities.

We should pause here to note that incorporating other cultural traditions into your household activities doesn't mean you have to permanently change your own traditions.

Nor does it mean you have to become hardcore world travelers or learn seven languages.

Rather, the point is to help your child simply recognize that other cultures have their own ways of doing things.

By familiarizing them (via repeated exposure at home) with the unique food, music, and dance moves of other cultures, it will make those cultural traditions seem less awkward and more ordinary.

A *moderate* representation of other countries' customs is enough. As long as it's fun and easy, it really doesn't take much for kids to integrate a new way of doing things into their routine.

Set an example

Here are some ideas for setting an example so your child can fully embrace your guidance.

Be aware of your own biases. If you behave in ways that demonstrate you're skeptical about the importance of cultural diversity, even though you say you're all for it, your child will notice and emulate your behavior.

Call out discrimination. If someone says or does something against other cultures in your own home and you don't intervene or say something in the moment, that will signal to your child that you're okay with that type of language or behavior.

Speak kind words. Whenever someone shares something about their culture with you (and your child is listening), you could say things like, "Wow, that is so interesting!" or "I didn't know that. I'm really glad you shared it with me." The goal is to teach your child how to treat people who have different cultural traditions from their own.

Promote cultural diversity with household surroundings

Here are lots of ideas for shaping your home environment to reflect the cultural diversity values you've been touting.

- **Media.** Talking about acceptance is a good first step, but it's not enough. Select movies, videos, TV shows, etc. that include characters from other cultures. Your media selection doesn't have to consistently include multicultural characters, but it's important that it never includes uncontested discrimination against other cultures. This might sound like an impossible task at first, but if you can start getting your family in the habit of choosing media based on fairness and acceptance and not based on a world where it's okay to discriminate, you'll be doing them an enormous favor. Try it.

- **Books.** Another idea for raising open-minded children is to fill your family bookshelf with kids' books about other cultures. Storylines that focus on other cultures are fine, but books that integrate people from other countries as a fundamental part of the storyline are even better.

- **Friends.** Friendships with people from other cultures can be one of the richest, most authentic learning experiences. Sharing a meal together, going on adventures, inviting one another to special cultural events familiarizes them with your culture and exposes you to *their* culture. The goal is to help children associate people from other cultures with the warm characteristics of friendship: human connection and kindness.

- **Music.** One of the better ways to make music fun for kids is to play a music game with the music of a world country playing in the background. Or you could even plan a meal from another country while playing that country's music. Get creative!

- **Food.** Instead of a normal Tuesday taco night, make it even more fun with miniature world toothpick flags. Let your kids decorate their food before they dig in. If they like the idea, ask them for suggestions for other international food they could decorate with world toothpick flags (pizza, waffles, Chinese dumplings, etc.) so they feel like they're part of the fun. Repeat the meals that are successful.

- **Language.** Whenever you use terms like "deja vu," be sure to mention the language it comes from (French). You could take the concept further by explaining that lots of foreign language terms are embedded in the English language. For example, the word *cookie* is a Dutch word, *ketchup* is Chinese, and *cartoon* is Italian. Be sure to praise your child for using words from other cultures in their daily language (this will hopefully encourage them to learn more).

- **Clothes:** You could wear clothing from another culture, but it doesn't have to be an entire outfit. Even if you're just wearing your robe, mention that American robes originated from Japanese kimonos. Or if you're wearing a raincoat/poncho—remember to call out South American clothing.

- **Art.** Give your child a piece of paper and colored pencils (or crayons) and ask them to draw a "diversity flower" with different-colored petals (or a train or whatever). If your child is really into art, suggest they make a collage of different cultures around the world. Origami? Sidewalk chalk art? Or you could *display* art in your home that was created by someone from another culture. Place the artwork somewhere that's seen by the whole family every day. Talk about what it means to you.

- **Trivia:** Most kids are fascinated by weird facts—go figure! Hopefully facts from other cultures will be equally captivating.

- **Memory game:** Have your kids create cards of international flags and then make it a game for them to name the country represented on each card. The cards can be printed, but kids might have more fun using colored markers/crayons to draw the flags on the cards. You could point out the different countries (represented by the flags they draw) on a map or globe, so your child has a sense of where the countries exist on our planet.

HOW TO RAISE INCLUSIVE CHILDREN

- **Virtual travel:** Traveling to foreign countries on the internet has gotten incredibly realistic (plus it's free!)—it's almost like you're actually there. And what kid isn't fascinated by castles and palaces in other countries? You could do a search on YouTube for "virtual world travel for kids"—there are tons of choices.

- **Family mission statement.** Things you say to your kids all the time can have an enormous impact on how their opinions form as they grow. Keep saying things like "we believe in justice for all cultures" or "we believe in respecting *all* humans, regardless of where they were born"— anything that denotes fairness and acceptance. It will sink in eventually.

- **Aromas**. Attend or participate in a cultural festival and take time to appreciate all the smells of different cultures, including spices, perfumes, incense, and food. It all comes together here. You could light a candle at home that mimics the aroma you experienced together. (Fun fact: the brain's memory and emotion functions are directly linked to the area of the brain that processes scent.)

Of course, there's more you can do to teach your child the value of cultural diversity. But any of the activities above will plant the seeds needed to help your child learn more about world culture.

Let them help you plan the activities, so they feel like they're part of the solution. Remember, the whole point is to make learning about other cultures fun!

Note: You can find most of the resource materials for the activities mentioned above for free or for around $5-$10 at your local party or art supply store, Dollar Store, Etsy, or Amazon.

Make the importance of cultural diversity an ongoing conversation

Teaching the importance of cultural diversity is not a once-and-done conversation. Issues will come up all the time that your child (hopefully) feels comfortable sharing with you.

As any parent knows, getting a concept to sink in with our kids needs to be repeated over and over (and over!) again.

Keep guiding them toward fairness and acceptance. Children need constant help understanding why each situation is either fair or unfair.

Children are a work in progress. Conversations about the importance of cultural diversity need to be a work in progress too.

Talking about fairness and acceptance repeatedly might feel cumbersome to you, but it hopefully doesn't to your child. They're progressively applying what you tell them to scenarios in their own life and deciding if it makes sense or not.

Depending on their attention span, who knows when you will say or model the right words at the right time. Keep trying. Plan for a marathon, not a sprint.

If they ask you a completely off-the-wall question about someone from another culture, don't panic. We'll cover common kids' questions about other cultures and how to answer them next.

Step 4. Learn How To Answer Kids' Questions About Other Cultures

If your child hasn't already met someone from another culture, it's more than likely they will at some point. Prepare yourself. Your curious child will no doubt have a lot of questions.

HOW TO RAISE INCLUSIVE CHILDREN

Let's go over some of the uh... "creative" questions that kids come up with and how to answer them.

Q: Why is that man wearing a cloth on his head?

A: *"It's called a turban, and he's most likely from India where it's common."*

Q: What's forced marriage?

A: *"Forced marriage is when someone (male or female) is pressured to get married when they don't want to."*

Q: Was pizza really invented in Italy?

A: *"Yes, pizza was first invented in Naples, Italy."*

Q: Why do people from other countries wear different clothes?

A: *"People from other countries wear different clothes because of their culture's traditions and also the weather."*

Q: Why is that woman wearing a scarf on her head?

A: *"It's called a hijab and she's most likely Muslim."*

Q: Why do Asian people have slanted eyes?

A: *"The evolution of the Asian eye started many generations ago, and no one knows for sure why it began."*

Q: What else do they eat in Japan besides sushi?

A: *"Japanese people eat a lot of fish, meat, rice, and vegetables, and it isn't always prepared as sushi.*

Q: Is our culture the best?

A: *"Every culture is different, and there's not one that's the best."*

Q: Jodi says her dad is Polish and her mom is Korean. Which parts of her are from which parent?

A: *"Polish and Korean, together, make up who Jodi is, but it doesn't separately affect different parts of her."*

Q: Why do some people eat bugs?

A: *"In some places, people eat bugs because they're a good source of protein. It might seem strange to us, but it's a normal part of their diet."*

Q: Can animals talk in other countries?

A: *"Animals can't talk anywhere, even in other countries."*

Q: Do people in other countries play the same games as us?

A: *"Some games are played all over the world, like hide-and-seek or tag. But there are also lots of different games that people play in different places."*

Q: Can I be friends with someone who is different from me?

A: *"Absolutely! One of the best things about being human is that we can learn from and enjoy people who are different from us."*

Q: Why does that person have brown skin?

A: *"Everyone has a different shade of skin. Even yours and mine are slightly different. Let's look."*

Q: Do people in other countries have birthdays?

A: *"Yes, people all over the world celebrate birthdays!"*

Q: Why is that boy wearing a dress?

A: "He's most likely Muslim, and some Muslim boys wear prayer dresses as part of their religion."

Q: Why does Ezra wear that little round thing on his head?

A: "It's called a kippah (or a yamaka), and Ezra wears it because he's Jewish."

TRISH ALLISON

Reference Notes

1. Bright Horizons, *Answering Your Child's Toughest Questions*, accessed 10 May 2025, <https://www.brighthorizons.com/article/children/answering-childrens-toughest-questions>.
2. Milford Kids Thrive, *Teachable Moments in Your Everyday Life*, accessed 10 May 2025, <https://milfordkidsthrive.org/teachable-moments-in-your-everyday-life/ >.
3. National Institute of Health (NIH), *Unhealthy Interactions: The Role of Stereotype Threat in Health Disparities,* accessed 10 May 2025, <https://pmc.ncbi.nlm.nih.gov/articles/PMC3518353>.

1. Learning for Justice, *Ten Myths About Immigration*, accessed 10 May 2025, <https://www.learningforjustice.org/magazine/spring-2011/ten-myths-about-immigration>
2. Learning for Justice, *Test yourself for hidden bias*, accessed 10 May 2025, <https://www.learningforjustice.org/professional-development/test-yourself-for-hidden-bias.>
3. McNulty, Carol, *Family Connections: Family Conversations in Informal Learning Environments,* Childhood Education, accessed 10 May 2025, < https://www.tandfonline.com/doi/abs/10.1080/00094056.2012.662136?journalCode=uced20>.
4. Resources for Early Learning, *Engaging Children in Meaningful Conversation*, accessed 10 May 2025, <http://resourcesforearlylearning.org/educators/module/20/7/19/>.
5. Gagne, Claire, 2020, Today's Parent, *Age-by-age Guide to Getting Your Kid to Talk to You,* accessed 10 May 2025s, <https://www.todaysparent.com/family/age-by-age-guide-to-getting-your-kid-to-talk>.

6. Center for Parenting Education, *The Skill of Listening*, accessed 10 May 2025, <https://centerforparentingeducation.org/library-of-articles/healthy-communication/the-skill-of-listening/≥>.
7. Price Genealogy, *Why it's important to teach your kids about genealogy*, accessed 10 May 2025, <https://www.pricegen.com/its-important-teach-kids-genealogy/>

1. A Colgan, C. A. & Lai, B. S., 2019, Info About Kids, *How to talk to your child about immigration: Recommendations for Parents*, accessed 10 May 2025, <https://infoaboutkids.org/blog/how-to-talk-to-your-child-about-immigration-recommendations-for-parents/>.
2. The Journal of Neuroscience, *Language Exposure Relates to Structural Neural Connectivity in Childhood*, accessed 10 May 2025, <https://www.ncbi.nlm.nih.gov/pmc/articles/PMC6125810/[1].>
3. Bright Horizons, *Talking with Children About Poverty and Homelessness*, accessed 10 May 2025, <http://brightspaces.org/wp-content/uploads/Talking-with-Children-About-Homelessness-Final.pdf>
4. The Homeless Hub, *How can we talk to young children about homelessness?*, accessed 10 May 2025, < How can we talk to young children about homelessness? | The Homeless Hub[2]>
5. Huffington Post, Talking to Kids About Homelessness, accessed 10 May 2025, <Talking to Kids About Homelessness | HuffPost Life[3]>
6. Brinda, Mary et al, 2016, *Role of Parents in Inculcating Values,*

---

[1]. https://www.ncbi.nlm.nih.gov/pmc/articles/PMC6125810/%20

[2]. https://www.homelesshub.ca/blog/how-can-we-talk-young-children-about-homelessness

[3]. https://www.huffpost.com/entry/talking-to-kids-about-homelessness_b_6473290

National Conference on Value Education, accessed 1 October 2020, <http://ijariie.com/AdminUploadPdf/ROLE_OF_PARENTS_IN_INCULCATING_VALUES_c1264.p>

7. Harvey, Jennifer. *Raising White Kids: Bringing up Children in a Racially Unjust America*, J Harvey - 2017 - books.google.com[4]

8. Rappaport, Lisa, 2018, Reuters Health, *Back-and-forth Conversations with Young Kids*, accessed 10 May 2025, <https://www.reuters.com/article/us-health-childhood-language/back-and-forth-conversations-with-young-kids-may-aid-brain-development-idUSKBN1KY28O>.

1. Welcoming Schools, *Defining LGTBQ Words for Children*, accessed 10 May 2025, <https://www.welcomingschools.org/resources/definitions/youth-definitions/>.

1. Brinda, Mary et al, 2016, *Role of Parents in Inculcating Values*, National Conference on Value Education, accessed 10 May 2025, <http://ijariie.com/AdminUploadPdf/ROLE_OF_PARENTS_IN_INCULCATING_VALUES_c1264.p>

2. New York University, Science Daily, *Implicit bias against women: Men more likely than women to be seen as brilliant*, accessed 10 May 2025, <https://www.sciencedaily.com/releases/2020/07/200702100533.htm>

3. Unicef, *Girls spend 160 million more hours than boys doing household chores every day,* accessed 10 May 2025, <https://www.unicef.org/press-releases/girls-spend-160-million-more-hours-boys-doing-household-chores-everyday>

4. Johnson, Nicole, Parent Map, *Equal Pay for Equal Chores. No, Our Kids' Value Isn't Based On Gender*, accessed 10 May

---

4. https://www.google.com/books/edition/Raising_White_Kids/DijuuAEACAAJ?hl=en

2025, <https://www.parentmap.com/article/equal-pay-equal-chores-no-our-kids-value-isnt-based-gender>
5. Carlzon, Becky, Learning Power Kids, *Let Children Lead*, accessed 10 May 2025, <https://learningpowerkids.com/giving-children-ownership/>.
6. Young, Karen, Hey Sigmund, *Teaching Kids How To Set & Protect Their Boundaries Against Toxic Behavior*, accessed 10 May 2025, <https://www.heysigmund.com/teaching-kids-how-to-set-boundaries-and-keep-toxic-people-out/>.
7. Parent.com, *5 Ways Boredom Makes Your Kid More Awesome*, accessed 10 May 2025, <https://www.parent.com/5-surprising-benefits-of-letting-your-children-get-bored/>.
8. Greenpath Financial Wellness, *Teaching Children How to Budget*, accessed 10 May 2025, <https://www.greenpath.com/teaching-children-how-to-budget/>.
9. Price-Mitchell, Marilyn, Roots of Action, *What is a Role Model? Five Qualities that Matter to Youth*, accessed 10 May 2025, <https://www.rootsofaction.com/role-model/>.
10. Bright Horizons Education Team, Bright Horizons, *Teaching Grit and Perseverance to Children*, accessed 10 May 2025, <https://www.brighthorizons.com/article/children/encouraging-grit-and-teaching-perseverance-to-children>.
11. Girish, Rati Ramadas, Get Litt, *Importance of Writing Skills for Children*, accessed 10 May 2025, <https://www.getlitt.co/blog/importance-of-writing-skills-for-children/>.
12. La Petite Academy, *Modeling Empathy for Children*, accessed 10-May-2025, <https://www.lapetite.com/blog/2018/03/modeling-empathy-for-children/>
13. Young, Karen, Hey Sigmund, *Teaching Kids How To Set & Protect Their Boundaries Against Toxic Behavior*, accessed

10-May 2025, <https://www.heysigmund.com/teaching-kids-how-to-set-boundaries-and-keep-toxic-people-out>.[5]

14. Carlzon, Becky, Learning Power Kids, *Let Children Lead*, accessed 10 May 2025, <https://learningpowerkids.com/giving-children-ownership>.

15. Wallace, Carey, Time Magazine, *How to Talk About Other Religious Traditions to Your Kids*, accessed 10 May 2025, <https://time.com/4052046/how-to-talk-about-other-religious-traditions-to-your-kids/>[6]

16. Dhenin, Marianne, Parents, *Millennial Parents Are Raising Their Kids Without Religion,* accessed 10 May 2025, <https://www.parents.com/parenting/better-parenting/teaching-tolerance/kids-respecting-other-religions/)>

17. Scholastic, *Holidays: A Sampler From Around the World,* accessed 10 May 2025, <https://www.scholastic.com/librarians/tech/ift_worldholidays.htm>

18. Hospice of the Piedmont, *Benefits of Seniors and Young Children Spending Time Together*, accessed 10 May 2025, https://www.hopva.org/blog/benefits-of-seniors-and-young-children-spending-time-together/

19. Kashef, Ziba, Baby Center, *How to talk to your child about disabilities (ages 5-8)*, accessed 10 May 2025, <https://www.babycenter.com/0_how-to-talk-to-your-child-about-disabilities-ages-5-to-8_3657045.bc>

20. Hutton, Lindsay, 2019, Family Education, *6 Tips to Talk to Your Kids About Disabilities*, accessed 10 May 2025, <https://www.familyeducation.com/life/empathy/6-tips-talk-your-kids-about-disabilities?slide=2%23fen-gallery%20>

21. Epling, Katy, Scary Mommy, *6 Ways To Teach Your Kids*

---

5. https://www.heysigmund.com/teaching-kids-how-to-set-boundaries-and-keep-toxic-people-out

6. https://time.com/4052046/how-to-talk-about-other-religious-traditions-to-your-kids/%3e

About Disabilities, accessed 10 May 2025, <https://www.scarymommy.com/disability-awareness-for-kids/>

22. Elbaum, Deborah M.D, care.com, *Teaching your child about peers with special needs*, accessed 10 May 2025, <https://www.care.com/c/stories/6618/teaching-your-child-about-peers-with-special/>

23. Kettle, Robin, Disabled World, *Wheelchair Etiquette and Disability Awareness*, accessed 10 May 2025, <https://www.disabled-world.com/disability/awareness/wheelchair-etiquette.php>

24. American Academy of Child and Adolescent Psychiatry, *Talking to Kids About Mental Illnesses,* accessed 10 May 2025, <https://www.aacap.org/AACAP/Families_and_Youth/Facts_for_Families/FFF-Guide/Talking-To-Kids-About-Mental-Illnesses-084.aspx>

25. Dr. Sidhu, Shawn, UNM Health Sciences, *The Importance of Siblings*, accessed 10 May 2025, <https://hsc.unm.edu/news/news/the-importance-of-siblings.html>

26. Dr. Beurkens, Nicole, Child Psychologist, *Here's What Siblings of Special-needs Kids REALLY Need*, accessed 10 May 2025, <https://www.drbeurkens.com/heres-what-siblings-of-special-needs-kids-really-need/>.

27. Hirsch, Larissa MD, Kid's Health, *Caring for Siblings of Kids with Special Needs,* accessed 10 May 2025, <https://kidshealth.org/en/parents/siblings-special-needs.html>

28. Price Genealogy, *Why It's Important to Teach your Kids About Genealogy*, accessed 10 May 2025, <https://www.pricegen.com/its-important-teach-kids-genealogy/>

www.ingramcontent.com/pod-product-compliance
Lightning Source LLC
Chambersburg PA
CBHW050649170426
43200CB00008B/1224